STRANGER ON THE SHORE

Stranger on the Shore

A personal struggle with renewal
and inner healing

ANTHONY ROSE

THANKFUL BOOKS

First published 2008

Published by Thankful Books
c/o P.O. Box 2118, Seaford BN25 9AR.

ISBN: 978 1 905084 17 3

Book design and production for the publisher by
Bookprint Creative Services, <www.bookprint.co.uk>
Printed in Great Britain.

CONTENTS

FOREWORD BY DAVID PYTCHES

I am delighted to commend this little publication.

In his recent popular book *Velvet Elvis*, Rob Bell relates how he found himself catapulted into the leadership of a very large congregation that had gathered around him with his vision for planting a new kind of twenty-first century church. He tells how, in the midst of all this excitement and doubtless his dealing with the problems of so many others, he is surprised to discover that he himself had a major hang-up that had never been properly resolved. This, of course, is not an uncommon experience for leaders. In the inner journey of one's life new situations throw up new challenges with fresh personalities to cope. But they also throw up new insights into one's own life. These can become quite a handicap in one's dealings with others and in one's relationship with the Lord, if not seriously confronted.

In a similar manner this book by Anthony Rose is a very honest revelation of one church leader's inner struggles, and the practical approach he has developed for tackling them – an approach which he readily shares with his readers in the hope, and with the prayer, that this could help them too. And I commend the book because I believe the mix of problem and solution in such a personal story would be appealing to anyone.

This lightly written book is easy to read. It is a very personal story told in a reflective rather than directive way, to encourage others to face up to their own hang-ups.

I hope many will read it and be blessed by it.

David Pytches
(Former Anglican Bishop of Chile, Bolivia and Peru, and founding leader of New Wine)

ACKNOWLEDGEMENTS

There are some people I very much want to thank for helping me in the journey that has led to the completion of this book. First, David Pytches for his support, encouragement and advice. Then those friends and family members who have supported me over the years, even when maybe they didn't know all the details of my story. Heartfelt thanks are due especially to my wife Jane, who has stuck by me through so much and still puts up with me. Above all, I want to thank him whose hand is upon my life and who ultimately makes me *me*.

INTRODUCTION

This book has been many years emerging. For a long time I've wanted to put down on paper my thoughts about my life and the various difficulties I've had in the past, caused in great part by the break-up of my parents' marriage when I was a child. I suppose it's been important to me personally to set things down, to go through them systematically and at least have some sort of record for posterity. However, my main reason for doing this is that I want to share with others what I think I've learned and am still learning about how human emotions work, in the hope that it will help others.

In my years as a Christian church leader I've come across many people struggling with similar difficulties and have tried to guide them to the best of my ability. It's not my intention to imply that everyone has serious emotional problems. However, no one is perfect and we all have something to learn about ourselves as we go through this journey we call life.

A huge number of books are accessible to ordinary people in the field of emotions and 'bettering yourself'. Many of these assume nothing spiritual, whereas others stray into all kinds of belief systems, often lumped together under the label New Age. In Christian circles too there have been many books published in recent times, often very helpful. My intention is not to produce a textbook; I'm not qualified to do that anyway. I certainly don't want to pretend to be what I'm not. I'm not a professional counsellor or psychologist. I often think a church leader is a bit of a jack of all trades really, gaining a little information about a lot of things ranging from church architecture to the workings of the human mind – oh, and with a smattering of biblical knowledge thrown in. Rather like a medical GP, if we think something needs more specialised knowledge we seek help from others.

So if I'm guilty in this book of appearing to be just an amateur psychologist, my apologies in advance. More seriously, I hope no one is led astray or damaged in any way. As with what anybody says or advises about emotional situations, ideas and advice have to be weighed up carefully and set against the ideas and advice of others. I shall refer in passing to other books, but only to those I have found personally helpful and not in any great number I have to say.

What you have here is in fact a personal story. Obviously the more you relate to that, the more you will get out of the book. It may be that your own parents split up when you were a child, or there were difficulties in your relationship with a parent. It may simply be that you've no idea why you feel the way you do. We're all different, and our characters and personalities have been formed in many different ways. I'll be thinking about some of these as we go along, but inevitably a lot of what I say will be coloured by my own experience.

The important thing for me is not just that many people I come across have difficulty with feeling depressed, anxious, shy, unable to relate properly to others or whatever. No, the problem goes a step back from that. It's actually that many people can't even identify what it is they feel. They are like the 'stranger on the shore' who feels lost, perhaps longing to be in another place spiritually or emotionally but feeling they can never actually get there. This is especially true for men, although not exclusively so. It's certainly part of my testimony and I'll be talking about this at some length. In fact, I want to argue that we *all* need to step back sometimes and take stock of our feelings and our personalities. We don't necessarily have to feel there's a specific 'problem' with ourselves, but the fact is that nobody's perfect. Just to consider, at least to an extent, what makes us the sort of person we are is always a useful exercise.

My story is inevitably written from the point of view of a follower of Jesus Christ for that is what I am, although much of what I have to say could be applied to anyone's life, whatever their beliefs. It's also written by someone who is convinced of the living power of the Holy Spirit to renew us. Again, many books have been written about Holy Spirit renewal. I'm committed to the whole idea of the need for God's church in our world to be renewed by the power of his Spirit. I will speak about how this has been a part of my life virtually since becoming a Christian.

As a church leader I've been committed to leading churches into renewal. This involves all sorts of things, including introducing people to the gifts of the Holy Spirit. True renewal in the Spirit, however, is not just about receiving gifts. It's certainly not just about external expressions such as worshipping more freely, important as these may be. True renewal is about allowing God's Spirit to do his work at every level of your being. I believe it will mean going deeper in the supernatural, in worshipping supernaturally and exercising mission and ministry in the same supernatural manner that Jesus did when he walked upon the earth. In order to be free to receive the full blessings of all this, we also need to be prepared for the Holy Spirit to do his sovereign work as the great Physician in our lives.

This is a lifelong work, for the Bible makes it clear that although Christians are assured of our salvation, no one will be perfect until changed 'in the twinkling of an eye' on the great Day of the Lord. Meanwhile, we're being changed slowly. The Spirit, if we allow him, is changing us to be like Jesus. Many people think that this is to do with our moral character, the way we behave and so on. This is quite right, but it's also much more than that. So often we're prevented from behaving as we should because of conflicts within ourselves, because of emotional disabling. More seriously perhaps, these conflicts not only mar our behaviour but they can actually spoil what is meant to be a beautiful relationship with our Lord and Saviour. Consequently we simply don't enjoy life as it's meant to be. Jesus said 'I have come that they may have life, and have it to the full.' (John 10:10). Does that describe your life or are there things that are unresolved in it?

Writing this book has not been an easy task. Obviously there's the whole business of having to revisit painful experiences such as the actual breakup of my parents' marriage or seeking professional help later on. There's wanting to get things right, of remembering details from many years ago. Above all, it's laying myself open and speaking about things that not even many people quite close to me knew about. As I'll be exploring to an extent, there's the whole belief people can have that being a Christian means you shouldn't have such problems. Being a church leader is even more difficult – you don't really want to show people your weaknesses.

Yet aren't such attitudes a denial of the very Gospel itself? The Good News Christians proclaim is that Jesus Christ saves you from your sin and the judgment that incurs. More than that, though, he saves you from your very self. The Christian Church is meant to be a community. Part of what that's about is to share each other's burdens. When one part of the body suffers, the whole body suffers. Yet much of the time Christians are afraid to open up and be truthful about their feelings. If only we could be more honest we might be surprised. As C.S. Lewis once said, 'Friendship is born at the moment when one person says to another, "What! You too? I thought I was the only one." '

An obvious thing about telling your own story is that you have to talk about yourself a lot. It doesn't sit comfortably with me having to use the words 'I' and 'me' all the time. As I hope will become clear, that's because my story isn't really about me at all; it's about the One who is renewing me. One of my main

arguments about inner healing is that it can only come ultimately when we are not centred upon ourselves but upon
Jesus. I want him to get the glory. Discovering him more will
mean discovering yourself more. The two always go together.
My hope and prayer therefore are that during the reading of
this book your eyes also will be lifted to him.

CHAPTER ONE

THE START OF THE JOURNEY

This can't be!

'What do you want me to do for you?'

I'm sure it wasn't intended, and maybe it was because of how I felt at the time, but the voice seemed intimidating and the question more than a little threatening. The consulting room was fairly small, not particularly welcoming, but I wasn't in the mood for noticing very much anyway. There was one chair for me, facing a rather daunting middle-aged consultant psychiatrist in a suit and half a dozen young medical students. I shifted uncomfortably, trying to look cool as I held my half-drunk coffee in its plastic cup. I was here voluntarily, but already wishing I was somewhere else.

But what on earth *was* I doing here? I was a reasonably mature Christian (so I thought anyway); someone who had been in church leadership with young people; someone who had played his guitar and sung in evangelism, who'd led worship in church. I thought I was the sort of person others could come and talk to about *their* problems. What's more, I was engaged to be married to a lovely girl, doing reasonably well working for a degree in a good university, having held down a responsible job in the Civil Service. Yet here I was, about to try to put into words in front of a group of complete strangers what my mind and emotions were going through.

16

This couldn't be! I really shouldn't be here, I thought. I can handle these feelings, surely?

The very word 'psychiatrist' summed up thoughts of failure. The problem was, I really needed help. My feelings were getting the better of me and I knew I had to do something – anything – to get sorted out. I believed in a God who answers prayer, who heals by the power of his Spirit. I'd had people pray with me. Yet I was struggling with unresolved emotional difficulties that I wasn't prepared to live with for the rest of my life.

So I had finally found myself here, having been referred by my GP who obviously thought I was genuine and perhaps spotted certain danger signs. To this day I don't know what she wrote, I only know my notes said something about 'anxiety'. That must be a term that covers a multitude of problems. The anxiety was in turn making me depressed and although I was making a good job of hiding it, it was causing life to be pretty miserable. I wasn't great company to those around me either.

His first question wasn't what I expected. When you go to the doctor he or she usually asks, 'What seems to be the problem?', and so you proceed to explain the symptoms in the hope that they'll have a look at you, make a diagnosis and recommend an effective treatment. But to be asked 'What you want me to do for you?' seemed a bit strange. I can't remember the exact answer I gave, but something along the lines of 'I want you to make me better!' might have been appropriate. I know that when I explained my feelings and how unhappy they were making me it was obviously enough to convince the consultant I was worth spending time on.

How did I get here?

The year was 1977. I was twenty-three years old. I'd left school with a couple of A levels five years before that and worked in the Department of Health and Social Security in Birmingham, where I grew up. I had lacked the confidence to think that I could manage a higher education course, but eventually after four years I did think I could give it a go. I applied to Birmingham University to read English.

At the time I was still living with my mother, which always creates tensions when you're in your early twenties and really ready to leave. My life outside work revolved around my church friends, plus I had a fiancée in town. So, I went to university while still at home. The course I undertook involved relatively few lectures and seminars and a great deal of time on my own reading a lot of English literature. Probably not the best recipe for someone who was feeling the way I was.

So what was the problem? I was certainly aware of questions of self-confidence from earlier on in my life, but as I hope to explain later on I felt a lot of this had been dealt with. I put most of this down to the fact that my parents split up when I was eight years old, not having a father around, and so on. More difficult to deal with were feelings of being left out by other people, which did cause me problems at times with other people in the circles in which I mixed. Again, I thought I'd dealt with a lot of these and in any case they were related to specific stages of my life. The phase I was at now should have meant I was quite happy. The problem was being close to somebody in a way I never had been before.

Out of control?

There was no logic to it whatsoever, but every time my fiancée Jane was involved in something that I perceived to be fairly important and I couldn't be involved myself a kind of pain gripped me inside. The real problem was that I couldn't identify exactly what the feeling was. Was it fear? Anger? Jealousy? The truth is, it might have been all those at the same time but I found it really hard to identify them. Examples of situations are easier to give: a time when she served on an inquest jury, times that involved anything medical, a college course that involved a lot of contact time which mine didn't. Anything where I was in some way not involved or excluded. I know lots of people can feel left out of things but this was so bad it was making me feel almost physically ill.

It felt so hard to talk to other people about any of these things, probably because I thought I must be the only person in the world who felt them and I could offer no logical explanation for them. I worried that other people looking in from the 'outside' would find it hard to understand if they didn't feel those things themselves. I worried that other people might label me as basically a bit insane as a result, not to mention what other Christians might think when, as a believer, I was supposed to have joy in my heart. Even now, it's incredibly difficult to admit such things. Someone reading this with a slight knowledge of psychology might already want to make assessments. It was his relationship with his father. It was his relationship with his mother. His fiancée was some sort of mother figure. It was something in his early childhood. I'm sure the list could go on.

Can God really help me?

Probably the worst thing that faces anyone who admits to psychological problems is the fear that other people will simply want to avoid you. I don't know how much this is a cultural thing. I know that the British and other north Europeans are not particularly good at expressing feelings. I know that men find it hard to admit their needs. For years many Americans have been quite open about consulting their 'therapist'. Books about psychology, self-betterment and so on always seemed to originate in the United States. We British have been very suspicious of such things in the past. I'm glad to say this is changing. The problem for Christians is that we're yet another step of suspicion away from all this. We live in a society full of alternatives. There are different remedies, spiritual healing, weird and wonderful beliefs from all over the place. Christians, particularly those who regard themselves as Bible-believing, are very mistrustful of anything that seems to go outside a biblical framework.

Personally I regard the Bible as the inspired Word of God. It has much to say about the human condition and later in this book I want to talk about how my relationship with the author and subject of that book has helped me over the years. However, just as I would go to the doctor with a physical problem even though I believe in the power of God to heal, so too I believe Christians need to take into account the knowledge that God has given us so far into the workings of the human brain. To use human therapies in order to understand our emotions is not in itself a bad thing, *as long as* we discriminate wisely and filter everything through the Word of God[1].

The point for me was not that God couldn't heal me; I definitely believed he could. But even with praying for people's healing, it helps to know where or what the pain is. In the Gospel accounts of healings, Jesus usually seemed to know what the problem was. Certainly a doctor needs to know what a patient is feeling and where the problem seems to be in order to begin some sort of diagnosis. In my case, I clearly had problems about identifying the 'pain'. On top of that, I was a man. As I'll discuss later, there are many differences between men and women. One of them is that men often like to 'box' things up in their minds, to put things into neat 'files' and deal with them one at a time.

This is partly what I was trying to do with my feelings. I wanted to put them into a box and say to myself, and to the world, that overall I'm an OK guy. I've got things together. I'm reasonably successful in life and in my Christian faith. These feelings are confined to just one area of my life. Nobody needs to know about them. I can sort them out and when I have I can forget about them and so can anyone else who might happen to know about them. It was on that basis that I agreed to my GP's suggestion that I should see a specialist. I saw it as 'An area of my life in which there are difficulties', and the rest of me would cope.

Understanding myself

After that first consultation I was referred on to another clinic. This was an old building with a large hall in the centre and various rooms going off it. My interview this time was without any watching students, thank goodness. The psychiatrist was a young man, who put me at ease. Looking back, I think one of my difficulties was dealing with older men. It's one of the many things I've had to recognise in terms of self-image, and so on. Mind you, being middle-aged myself now I have to be careful I don't give the same problem to others. Being a vicar is even worse, considering some of the awful preconceptions people have about the clergy!

The original consultant had suggested group therapy, but it's something that didn't really appeal to me. Maybe it would have done me some good, but I was still suffering from this 'boxed up, go it alone' mentality and I asked if I could see someone individually. I honestly hadn't thought that the British National Health Service could stretch to it, but I was able to have an hour's consultation every week with this man all to myself. It was to last for the next eighteen months, until he thought I was able to cope. Apart from when my GP tried me on some pills for a while at the very beginning it was felt that in my case medication wouldn't help. I'm very aware that this is not always the case and sometimes people need drugs just to get themselves on an even keel.

The question is, did those eighteen months do me any good? As a church leader over the last few years I've worked alongside many people in different situations, often being called on to use what has amounted to counselling skills although I've never had formal training in them. When the problems have seemed very deep-seated, I haven't hesitated to suggest to people that they seek more ongoing counselling elsewhere. It seems wise to me to know your limitations, as well as when you're unable to give the time needed to someone. However, I have read what I can and picked up bits and pieces over the years. I know, for example, that the kind of therapy I received all those years ago is a type of counselling based on the work of Carl Rogers, known as Person-Centred or Client-Centred Therapy, which was developed in the 1940s and 50s. It is a very non-directive technique. The therapist never suggests a particular course of action. It's all based on the subject talking through the feelings, trying to express them freely, thereby discovering what they are and somehow denuding them of their power and influence. It's one form of therapy that has proved very popular over recent years. It doesn't have much to say about the spiritual. Indeed, Carl Rogers himself rejected the idea of God. But just as I pray for people to be healed supernaturally and advise them to seek medical help for physical problems, so I'm sure it's not a difficulty to seek psychological understanding within a certain framework *as long as* I allow for the possibility of divine intervention as well.

I have to say it took that year and a half of talking before I really began to understand things about myself. Actually I think I was never able to express completely freely the feelings within, always maintaining that shell of emotional protection I'd developed over years. However, one thing I learned very clearly during that time was that this was all about *me* – the whole me. It was not about something that was just a part, something belonging to a box, or like a dog in the corner that was simply barking too loudly. This was about the need for my whole personality to discover what made it tick in the process of getting healed.

This was the beginning of a road of self-discovery that was to continue well after therapy, and indeed continues today. Nobody is perfect. The Bible makes that very clear. In a famous passage, the Apostle Paul tells his readers that the perfect has not yet come:

> Now we see but a poor reflection as in a mirror; then we shall see face to face. Now I know in part; then I shall know fully, even as I am fully known. (1 Corinthians 13:12)

It will be a great day when we know fully, but for now our calling is to travel on the imperfect road towards it.

Watch out – God at work

These days, when I talk to anyone in my capacity as a church leader, I often find myself telling them not to be so hard on themselves, or to remember that we're in a fallen world in which we're currently being renewed and reconstructed. As a line on a T-shirt says: 'Please be patient, God hasn't finished with me yet.' We never actually take the L-plates off. It seems to me that the problem so many people have in their relationships with each other is that they're not ready to stop and take stock; to look at themselves with a bit of honesty and ask why they might feel the way they do. Indeed *what* is it they feel? Can they identify it; put it into words? And why are we different from each other? What causes tensions? Is it that people are simply different personalities or that they carry a lot of baggage, perhaps damage from way back in their past?

It's not that any of this is new. Books and books have been written about it. Not just academic textbooks but accessible popular works that have been targeted at those who want to understand. I have to admit that those are the ones I read, so I remain very much the non-expert! All I want to do, as I did back then, is to try to understand myself a little better. I'm always willing to learn more. Maybe others will be helped by what I've learned, but the key always is to be willing.

During the time I went each week to see a shrink (why do we call them that when the idea is to expand your mind?) I tried to look back at my past and discover what could have caused me to have the difficulties I had, in spite of my handicap of thinking too much in boxes. I thought perhaps I could identify certain traumatic experiences, not least of which must have been my parents splitting up, and link them to specific feelings. Simply by remembering, I would see them disappear.

It was not to be so. I had to face up to the fact that a whole number of things, many of which I might never remember, had contributed to my being the person I was. This was going to challenge the way I saw myself, my personal relationship with God, and my whole notion of renewal in his Spirit. The time was hard, especially because I felt able to share what I was going through with so few people.

Talk about it

When my parents split up in 1962 people didn't talk about that sort of thing too much. Divorce was still a dirty word. Nowadays, many of the younger people in our communities come from difficult home backgrounds. Our society is recognising that dysfunction in any family can lead to problems for people later in life. But in Christian circles there is still the tendency to preach a Gospel of triumphalism. When you come to Jesus, you're a new person (2 Corinthians 5:17). Just believe in Christ and all will be well. It can be very subtle. A church that preaches and practises a ministry of healing, that talks about and even demonstrates the power of God regularly, may actually make it harder to for some people to be truly honest.

Maybe I was wrong, but I found it incredibly difficult to admit my problems to other Christians. Why couldn't I accept what Jesus said? He was quite clear: 'It is not the healthy who need a doctor, but the sick.' (Matthew 9:12). We know that he reached out to those who recognised their need for him. The sick, the lame, the blind, the deaf, those who knew they were sinners, even the demonised all came to him and he set them free. The trouble is, if we're in a church that believes such things about healing we can easily fall prey to the success syndrome. We want to be seen to be a church where God is at work. We would like to be known as a place where people get healed, where God's presence and power are felt. And of course we want to be growing in numbers. A successful church is made up of successful members, and we mustn't admit that we are one of the less successful ones.

To me, true renewal in the Spirit is not about receiving gifts we impart to others and forgetting that God wants to deal with us too. To bear the Spirit of God within is to bear the pain He feels for the world and to find that He wants to deal with *our* pain, to make us more mature and to help us to become the people we're meant to be. That's rarely going to be easy. The question I had to face back then was whether I really wanted him to sort me out. Perhaps it was actually by his grace that I found the pain of my unresolved emotions too much to cope with. There wasn't a huge amount of choice in the end, unless I was prepared to end my engagement to be married. The pull of being in love with a fantastic girl was too great for that!

True renewal

'What do you want me to do for you?'

Why did that question seem so strange to me? After all, Jesus said the same thing. In Luke 18 a blind man shouts out for mercy. In Mark 10 he's named as Bartimaeus and he comes right up to Jesus. In Matthew 20 there are two men shouting out persistently. They're slightly different versions, but all agree that Jesus says to them, 'What do you want me to do for you?' Surely it was obvious to him? Maybe it was, but he needed to hear the reply. When it came ('I want to see!') he healed them. In another incident, Jesus asks a man paralysed for thirty-eight years if he wants to get well. What a daft question, we might think. Of course he does! Or does he? Sometimes when people have been in a certain condition for a long time it's actually hard for them to imagine what life could be like otherwise.

Sometimes people cling on to their sickness because it's somehow safe. How would they cope with suddenly being expected to do things they haven't been able to for such a long time? What if the healing process actually proves to be too painful? R.T. Kendall says, 'Many people don't want their problems solved, they only want them understood.' When that happens, it can lead to a lot of work for anyone trying help, but with little result because the subjects involved may be unable to contemplate actually moving on in maturity. Others may not even want their problem understood or, perhaps worse, they won't admit there's a problem in the first place.

Do we want to get better? Well, we're all on a journey of change if we're open to the Holy Spirit. Spiritual renewal has actually been a struggle for me, because it has involved all of me, not just a part. It took my being really close to another human being, with all that involved in terms of self-worth and so on, to bring my problems to the surface. You may not identify with my particular feelings. You may not need the kind of healing I'm talking about. The last thing I want to do is imply that everyone has problems for which they need to have counselling. But we all do need to change into Christ's likeness 'with ever-increasing glory' (2 Corinthians 3:18). To me, that means getting to know yourself better; being honest and true to yourself. It means understanding, as far as you can in this imperfect life, what makes you tick and perhaps what makes others the way they are so we can get on better. It's important to remember that we're all different, of course. Nothing I say in this book should be taken as a blueprint. It's my story, no one else's. I'm just asking you to come along on the journey as I describe what it's been like for me and what I think I've learned along the way. I've an awful lot to learn yet!

Who's the expert?

I'm also aware that many people struggle through depression and other conditions for physical reasons, where the brain is affected in some way. We need to know something about these, if not for ourselves then in order to help others. Once again, it's important to leave some things to those who know what they're doing. Perhaps the cause is chemical or hormonal (such as in post-natal depression) and medication is part of the answer[2]. Having said that, medical science still has a long way to go in understanding the brain, given what an incredibly complicated and wonderful organ it is. There are also many people who have been through far worse than I have. They may have had many more factors contributing towards the way they feel. I have known people over the years who have almost given up hope that they can be healed and set free.

The real question is whether we really do believe God can heal. The answer for me has to be 'yes', although it can take time, maybe even a lifetime. But it has to begin with honesty and with a genuine desire to be healed however painful the process of self-discovery may be. I said earlier that I thought I was a reasonably mature Christian when I found myself experiencing problems. Actually, I'd only been following Christ for around six years. Looking back I realise I was hardly getting going. Even now I have days when I feel anything but mature, and I've been a Christian for a lot longer. It's possible to shut the Spirit out at any time in your walk with God. But when you do let him have his way, you have to be prepared for new things to be revealed to you. God is always doing a new thing. About myself, I can only say to everyone, 'Please be patient, God hasn't finished with me yet!'

Notes

1. See Roger F. Hurding, *Roots and Shoots*, (Hodder & Stoughton, 1985) for an excellent critique of the various counselling and psychotherapy techniques.
2. I found the following book very useful for understanding something of how the body works in affecting our emotions: Dr John Lockley, *A Practical Workbook for the Depressed Christian*, (Authentic Lifestyle, 1991). The book is also excellent for allaying the fears and guilt of Christians who have depression or other needs and for providing very practical guidelines for healing.

CHAPTER TWO

STRANGER ON THE SHORE

Family line

My parents married just after the Second World War. My mother was from the Swansea Valley in South Wales. Her first language was Welsh. In 1940 she went to train as a primary school teacher in Dudley, West Midlands. As far as I can tell she was the first of her family to cross the great divide and fall in love with an Englishman. My father served in the Army during the War. He wouldn't talk about his wartime experiences when I was young but later he spoke about them just a little, mainly about Italy. Shortly after my parents were married he was posted to India for a while. Life was hard and uncertain in those days, but at least after the War there was a renewed hope and a sense of optimism.

Eventually, my parents bought a house in a middle-class suburb of Birmingham where my older brother and I were brought up. My father worked as a lithographic artist. My memories of early childhood are generally happy ones, with the usual recollections of holidays and indeed of a secure home. My father would come home from work every day. In the winter he would warm himself in front of the open fire and ask, 'Any news? Any mail?' To me as a child there was never any hint of the difficulties to come.

While I was Rector of two country parishes in Somerset I was always getting letters from people trying to trace their family trees from the parish records. I was usually relieved to be able to refer queries on to the County Records Office where older records were kept. For some reason the people who wrote to me often seemed concerned to tell me all the details of their family history. I'm sure it was fascinating for them! However, it did underline for me how important it can be for people to trace their family tree. People are searching for a sense of identity, and much of that will inevitably come from a sense of belonging to a family.

As a Christian, I know I really get my identity from being a child of God. However, none of us can escape some of the things we've inherited from our parents and ancestors. Because my parents split up when I was quite young it's been quite hard for me to have a sense of continuity on both sides of my family. As I think about what I want to say in this book it's become more important for me to trace back over not only my own history but the history of my family as well.

Some time ago I traced my Welsh family line back about 150 years, simply from chatting to two aunts. Mostly it went back to farming communities in Carmarthenshire. Being very proud of my Welsh heritage this was an important exercise for me. I never knew much about my father's side, although more recently a church member very kindly did some research on my family history. He managed to trace back my paternal line to my great great great great grandfather, born around the year 1771. Mostly it uncovered an ordinary Black Country working class background. It appears that Roman Catholicism 'entered the line' with my grandmother, but nothing is certain on that score.

After my father's death I was able to piece together something of a story. He had a hard childhood. My grandfather committed suicide when my father was about three years old and my father was sent to a Catholic boarding school from a very early age. I'd known about the suicide before, but never really thought enough about the effect on my father. He did well in art school. How I wish I'd inherited that particular talent! It's worth mentioning that his sister died when she was young. I find it hard to think that he was only seventeen when war broke out. How can someone of my generation understand what that might mean?

What effect any of this had on him I can only guess at, even more so what indirect effect it might have had on me as one of his children. It was helpful talking to my half sister and half brother in more recent times. They knew him at a later age than me. However, I can't speak with any real insight about how I was treated as a young child emotionally by my father. My main story has to be about what happened when I was eight years old.

'Dad's leaving us'

There can't be any right way of telling a child that their parents are splitting up. I think I was in my bedroom at the time. I remember my mother being in tears and wondering what was wrong. She said quite simply, 'Dad's leaving us.' I can't remember what was said immediately after that by anybody, but I know there were lots and lots of tears. My brother was three years older than me. Needless to say he took it badly as well. There was no way I was going to understand about the problems married couples can have. All I know is that there was undoubtedly an element of self-blame on my part. What could I possibly have done, maybe along with my brother, to cause my dad to want to leave? I certainly remember one occasion not long before that when my brother and I were having an argument in the back of the car. My dad stopped the car to tell us off. Was I really that bad a human being? Having told my own children off on many occasions I know I was no worse than anyone else. At the time, my child's mind saw things differently.

It turned out that my father had been having an affair with a woman from his office for some time. My mum had known about it for a year but I suppose had hoped that things might somehow work out. Apparently my father declared that he loved both women in his life. I'm not qualified to say if this is possible but I guess it wouldn't be the basis of a particularly good marriage! How my mum had managed to hide this from my brother and me I'll never know.

The weeks that followed the announcement were not good ones as you can imagine. My mother was devastated. I remember carrying on doing the things children do: playing with my friends out in the street or in the back garden, playing with my toys in my room, watching television. I suppose children are just better at distracting themselves than adults. Of course, all the time this terrible situation was in the background.

The fact is, fear lurked like some awful monster in the background. Up until then everything had seemed relatively certain – home was a secure place, there would always be family holidays, while the future was something you didn't have to think about very much at my age. Now things were different. There *was* a future to face and it was a bit like staring into a big black cloud. You couldn't possibly see how it was going to work out.

So it was that I carried on with the sort of dual thinking that helped me to survive as an eight year-old. I remember talking about it with my brother, but he was hardly in a position to analyze the situation any more than me. Memories are funny things. As I try to recollect those weeks and months back in 1962 I know there's a danger of embellishing memories. I think I tried to talk to my dad about things but I can't remember too well. What I do remember vividly was what was on television and what was in the music charts at the time. I'm a child of my generation after all!

On the television a BBC children's drama series called *Stranger on the Shore* had been running. It was about a French au pair girl living in England – she was the stranger on the shore. The closing credits rolled over film of her standing on the beach looking out to sea towards France, while Acker Bilk's hit theme of the same name played. It was a haunting clarinet piece. To her dying day my mother could never listen to that tune, and I still associate it with the time in question. It didn't help that my father had at one time been learning to play the clarinet himself and even used to play the tune. There were lots of other popular songs around; my mum could never listen to 'Moon River' either, but 'Stranger on the Shore' was the one that really stuck out for us.

That's why I decided to give this chapter (and the book) the title I have. When things happen to you that affect you at the deepest emotional level you can't simply dissect them rationally. For a young child it's even harder. You're far more likely to respond by remembering feelings even if you can't describe them. It's likely that you also associate circumstances or external stimuli with the traumatic period in question. For me it was a popular tune of the time. Others might remember a movie or a particular news event. Of course, some people can react in the opposite way, blanking out things or being so deeply upset that they're unaware of the world around.

It occurs to me that 'stranger on the shore' is very apt also as a description of my life in those dark days. In many ways I too was staring out across a sea, somehow not feeling I belonged and longing to be 'home', wherever that was. As we'll see later, in terms of feelings I was to become a bit of a stranger to myself.

Left out

I've only been describing how I remember my parents announcing they were splitting up. I can't recall everything, and they must have tried to shield us boys as much as they could. I do remember one or two events. My mother and father announced at some point that he wasn't going to leave after all and my brother and I jumped around for joy. Quite why hopes were raised like that I'll never know. I suppose it shows he was a man in turmoil really. Anyway, it was short-lived and it wasn't long afterwards that my father actually did leave. I don't remember his going, just that he didn't come home from work any more.

I also remember a big family conference at some point. A friend of the family stayed in the living room with my brother and me while my parents met in the front room with my mother's parents up from Wales and my father's mother there as well. Years later my mother told me how close she had been to her mother-in-law and how hard it was for all of them as my grandmother inevitably was forced to 'take sides' to a degree. Of course, I don't know that she really took sides. I don't think she was at all happy with what my father was doing, but as a mother she naturally would have had protective instincts. The situation itself simply meant my mother lost contact with a friend.

While that meeting was going on I can remember an overwhelming feeling of helplessness. To a degree, I also felt left out. Wasn't what I felt important? Didn't anyone care about my opinion in the matter? I guess anger must have been an important emotion at the time. I'm sure those feelings would prove significant in years to come. Rationally speaking one has to say that the feelings of my brother and I were probably discussed at length. I'm sure everyone, including my father, wanted to work things out for us. My father's problem was that he was having an affair and was caught in a kind of trap. He couldn't do what was best for us even if he wanted to. Well actually he could of course, if his will had been strongly inclined enough. The problem is, so strong is the pull the wrong way in such situations that willpower and rational thought can go out of the window[1].

I fear that my dad may have been trying to justify his actions at the time in a way that many more people do today. 'It's OK, kids are stronger than you think. They'll get over it. We can both see them just as much as before,' and so on. I simply want to say as firmly as I can that I don't believe that's true! Children are not super-resilient. God has given us the family as a gift – family where there is a father and a mother with different but complementary roles. Children need a mother and a father.

As I've seen my own children growing up this has become much clearer to me. Particularly seeing my son going through adolescence, I've been aware how much a boy needs a father. There is the whole issue of having a role model. There's the question of approval needed from an older male. In Christian circles we now talk quite openly about how knowledge of God as a heavenly Father can be affected by one's relationship with an earthly father. It's a key issue for many people.

Ironically, in recent years people have become more aware of all this despite the 'alternatives' being suggested and tried out. I really struggle with many of the ideas that are becoming prevalent. Alternative family structures are being hailed all the time, including adoption of children by same-sex couples. It may not be politically correct to say what I think, but we have yet to see the proof of these alternatives. I can only speak from my personal experience and the evidence I submit is contrary to what many are saying.

Many emotions

So, I was aware of some of my feelings at the time. Looking back I know there were many other emotions happening inside me too. I've mentioned the notion of guilt. An eight year-old isn't going to understand about how marriages work or not. As a child, my universe still centred on me to a large extent. Cause and effect in my world therefore were still very much based around me, not other people. The natural thing was to have an element of self-blame. I must have been a bad boy for my father to do such an extreme thing. I didn't verbalise this, but I know it was going on[2].

There was also a huge element of shame in the whole thing, which was to manifest chiefly in how I formed relationships at secondary school. Above all, though, there was this great sense of having my basic security taken away from me. A fear that in fact the whole world was somehow against me. It was a very big world, after all, and the one who should be there to help me face up to that world was no longer going to be, well, just *there*.

I think it's difficult for people who haven't been through this themselves to understand fully. These days many more families are experiencing break-up. Family courts are busy working out custody arrangements. Children are more often than not placed with their mothers, seeing their fathers at weekends. The danger in all this is that a false family situation is created. As my children grow up they do their own thing more and more. They don't want to spend every minute of the day around my wife and me. They like their own rooms (entertainment centres these days, actually!) and they like the freedom to go out. Even very young children like their 'independence', as long as Mum and Dad are around.

And that's the secret. You don't have to be doing things with your parents all the time, but you do want them to be *there*. I didn't want to spend all day every Saturday or Sunday doing stuff with my dad. Don't get me wrong; I loved doing things with him, as I think my kids have liked doing things with me. However, the chief thing was for him to be there; there when I needed him, there to show him something I'd just made, there to express an opinion to, there to help provide the boundaries to my behaviour, there simply for a hug.

I do hope that if you're a single parent reading this you're not feeling bad at my saying all this. The last thing I want is to make anyone feel guilty or inadequate. We live in a fallen world and our society has managed to create an environment where marriage is under threat more than it's ever been. That's certainly not to avoid apportioning blame, but I'm also acutely aware of how much guilt there is surrounding marriage break-up.

As time went by my mother was able to say things to me about how she felt. One of her emotions, apart from the obvious sense of loss, was a feeling that she was somehow deficient as a woman and a wife – that in a way it was *her* fault that her husband had chosen another woman. Dare I say it, but in some ways marriage break-up is worse than a spouse dying. Hope of reconciliation may be around for a while to cling to, but it will fade and the sense of loss will eventually be as great.

On top are a multitude of feelings other than grief. Shame, embarrassment, guilt and inadequacy can all be there. That's not to mention all the other stuff of love turning to hate and bitterness, feelings towards a 'rival', legal arguments, dividing the family possessions, what to do about the children. All a bit of a mess, really.

The best days of your life?

As I witness the progress of our children's education, I can't help but remember back over mine. After my father left, I think I carried on at primary school in much the same way as I always had. I was reasonably popular. Indeed, I was a bit of a leader in junior school. I often found myself heading up one side in 'battle' at lunchtimes whichever war scenario was being re-enacted.

Having said that, things at home were obviously affecting me. Deep down, I was hurting badly. I never spoke about it at school. My relationship with teachers was ambiguous. Did they know about my situation? They must have done, but no one ever talked to me about it. I do remember being in trouble with my class teacher once for talking when I hadn't seen him enter the room. Somehow he managed to slate my whole character in front of the entire class. At least, that's how it felt.

I suppose most people remember the times they got into trouble as children. What was different for me was that on this occasion my whole inside seemed to crumble. So I was not a very nice person after all. I don't know if I really believed that or not, but I'm certain it didn't help my self-confidence. I suppose I really felt very angry with the teacher for not understanding and for being, well, wrong about me. The point is I remember that particular incident as though it were yesterday.

It's obvious looking back that several things were going on inside me. One was an ambiguity towards authority. Without realising it I was becoming something of a rebel. I have read a lot about how people who have lost a father figure in their life can become delinquents, turned to drink and drugs, and so on. It wasn't that simple for me. Instead I became rather withdrawn and internalising a desire to kick against the world. I was angry all right, but that anger didn't have any way of expressing itself. I suppose really my self-confidence had gone.

Grammar school

When I went to secondary school any difficulties I may have had with self-confidence were accentuated. I had no permanent support in the form of an adult male. When my father left, my mother's family did all they could to support us. At first we had no car, and we'd travel every school holiday down to South Wales on the train. We'd change in Cardiff and be picked up at Neath by my uncle, actually my mother's brother-in-law. In the coming years he did his best to be a support, taking me to rugby matches and so on. He could never be the same as a father 'on the scene', though. When school holidays were over, we returned to Birmingham.

So it was that Wales became a second home in essence, and a place of security. Birmingham where is where I had to face the world. My secondary school was a boys' grammar, one of the 'better' ones. For me it was never an experience I really enjoyed. Actually, my perception was that it was all about 'the best'. The best boys were creamed off for the first fifteen rugby team at the very first sports lesson. Not me, I have to say; I was too small to be a forward and too short-sighted to be a back. I could hardly see a ball without glasses let alone catch it! I was put into an 'accelerated' class to do some O levels a year early and so get excellent A level grades and go to Oxford or Cambridge.

In fact, I think I was made to feel I was underachieving. Every term we were told our position in the form. I nearly always came seventeenth or eighteenth and my reports said I could do better. Maybe that was meant to be encouraging, but no one ever pointed out that I was in the top class of three and so was always seventeenth or eighteenth out of ninety, not thirty. I have to say my children's schooling has proved much more encouraging than that.

The worst thing for me about secondary school, however, was not feeling I could talk about my parents splitting up. No one else I knew there was in the same position. At least no one else admitted to it. There was too much shame involved. To tell others my parents were separated was just too much. In practice it meant I let very few other boys close to me. When I came to the end of term, we had to address the envelopes in which our reports were placed. I always wrote 'Mr and Mrs D.P. Rose' on mine. I know it broke my mother's heart that I felt as I did.

How times have changed! When I went to secondary school it was 1965. My school photo that year shows me on the front row in short trousers. My children can hardly believe I'd still be in those at the age of eleven. As far as I can ascertain, in those days divorce law meant that a five-year separation period had to pass by before a divorce could be granted, unless the injured party cited adultery. My mother never wanted to go through the latter. For a time therefore we were almost in a state of limbo; parents not divorced but not together either.

Self-confidence

Apart from the problems that surfaced later on, as I began to describe in chapter one, there were two that were very obvious as I entered adolescence: self-confidence and insecurity. Both are hardly surprising, I suppose, given the family situation. Later on, I want to talk about healing from these. For now I'll just say that both can be crippling. Self-confidence issues seem to be so widespread amongst people I've ministered to over the years.

As I entered my teenage years it seemed to get worse for me. I'm not a natural introvert and I enjoy mixing with other people and getting my 'energy' from them. However, those years were overshadowed by what had happened. I started to spend a lot of time on my own at home. We lived two bus rides away from school and somehow I lacked the confidence to travel to see friends outside school hours. In any case there was that shame factor I've spoken about and I didn't want them to come to my house. Whenever I went out, I was always tremendously self-conscious. I know this is a problem for many younger teenagers but for me it became almost crippling. Even answering the front door or running errands to the local shops became an effort.

When you become like that, the whole thing becomes a bit of a vicious circle. Everyone else seems to be more gregarious than you are. They all appear more confident. My brother seemed much more able to mix. He had school friends, mixed through Scouts and generally went out a lot. Even my mother got back on course with her social life. She was an extrovert and loved to be around people. She belonged to a church, she sang in a choir, acted in amateur dramatics and began to enjoy life. She never did marry again, despite having one or two suitors. I suppose the damage had been done on that score.

All this meant I was in the house on my own quite a lot. I longed to have a girlfriend but of course lacked the confidence to go anywhere to meet someone, let alone ask them out. I don't think it helped going to an all boys' school, but then others that went there didn't seem to have any problem at all so I'll keep off that argument.

At the age of fifteen I somehow became even more aware of my Welsh roots. I suppose this is hardly surprising given all I said about the emotional ties I had. This time the interest was towards Welsh rugby, which was very much on the up, and towards Welsh nationalism. It may seem crazy that somebody living in the Midlands could take such an interest. Actually Birmingham was full of Welsh people, quite a few in the teaching profession like my mother. Even the teacher I mentioned earlier was Welsh, but I didn't let that stop me!

I tried to take up rugby at school, but unfortunately I needed a lot more encouragement than I received. However, that didn't stop me watching the national team on television in its ascendancy. They were the glory days of Gareth Edwards, Barry John and the like. Although I only got to one international in Cardiff my uncle used to take me to see Neath, Swansea and Llanelli when they played London Welsh at Christmas and the Barbarians at Easter. That's how I got to see many of my heroes in the flesh.

The nationalism was even more serious. I became a fully paid-up member of Plaid Cymru, the Welsh Nationalist Party. My mind at that time was set on the idea of moving to Wales when I was older. Maybe I'd go to university there. Maybe I'd get involved in politics. Of course I'd have to learn Welsh since my mother hadn't spoken it to me as a child. As I describe later, no such plans were to become reality. Nevertheless, it was where I channelled my energy at the time. It was an emotional cause for me to get my teeth into. Call it a distraction if you like, but I suppose it gave me something beyond school and home. Teenage years are not really about entertainment; that's a mistake we seem to have made. No, those years are about longing for *adventure*. For me, here was a cause I could get really excited about.

For future aspirations it was very much a case of dreaming. I would have to wait a long time to put my newfound interests into practice. If truth be known, I couldn't really think that far ahead. In any case, I couldn't see how I was going to escape the confines of my own lack of self-confidence. I'm glad to say there's much more to the story, and things were to turn out very differently.

Notes

1. Willard F. Harley, *His Needs Her Needs*, (Monarch Publications, 1994) is an excellent book about marriage. In it, Harley likens having an affair to an addiction. As such, it is almost impossible to end it without completely breaking off contact with the other person.

2. I came across this telling quote in a BBC online guide (no longer available) to the law on divorce: 'Divorce can be especially confusing for children, who are likely to feel bewildered by events and may even blame themselves for their parents splitting up. So it is important to minimise the trauma suffered where possible.'

CHAPTER THREE

GETTING TO KNOW JESUS
Who makes me me? 1

A whole new challenge

I've often heard stories of dramatic conversions to Christianity. Sometimes people have been on drugs and been miraculously delivered. Sometimes they have been in prison and led terrible lives. When I first became a Christian I wished that I had such a dramatic story. I wanted to be the one maybe who had been on drugs, or slept around, or even been in trouble with the law. I wanted to be able to say how I'd been rescued from the most terrible depravity. People would listen to a story like that, wouldn't they?

Of course that was an extremely immature way of looking at things. There's nothing wrong with being ordinary! Indeed, I became a Christian at a relatively young age and I am enormously grateful that God rescued me from what I could have become.

Having said that, I can still say that things did change quite dramatically in my late teens. I've already said how self-confidence was a huge issue in my life. It must have worried my mother enormously. While my brother seemed to be having an extremely healthy social life, I looked pretty incapable of following in his footsteps. I wasn't a natural loner, far from it; I longed to have a girlfriend and be out mixing with kids of my own age. One day my mother arranged for a lad in our road to call for me and take me down to the local youth club. For me that was scary.

I remember walking into the place and feeling like a non-swimmer in the deep end of the swimming pool. However, it wasn't long before I became involved in the place and found myself playing badminton, table tennis and so on. I suppose you could look at my 'development' at that time and suggest that what happened was quite natural. At last I was involved in some friendships outside school. I got out of the house. I got a life! Self-confidence issues were bound to begin to be resolved as I came out of myself.

I don't deny there might be a great deal of truth in that. However, although I became involved in this youth club I still found it hard to form relationships, simply through shyness and inexperience. As it was there was to be an even greater challenge to me than simply the area of human relationships. It was all to do with how I discovered a relationship with the God who made me. I still love telling my story even if it isn't as dramatic as some.

We all have a spiritual pedigree, even if our parents were atheists. My pedigree was very mixed. My mother was a member of a Welsh Congregational Chapel. Indeed she never gave up that membership in all the years she lived in England. Her mother was strongly 'chapel', although her father was much more of an agnostic; maybe he didn't disbelieve in God altogether but he certainly wasn't sure about him. I've mentioned that there was Roman Catholicism in my father's background, but to my knowledge he never practised it as an adult and really could only be described as agnostic.

So where did that leave me? Because of my mum's faith I was encouraged from a young age to go to Sunday School at the local Baptist church she attended in Birmingham. It happened that the youth club I went to as a teenager was attached to that church, but that's later in the story. I heard all the stories about Jesus. In those days you even heard about him more at school. Mine was hardly what you'd call a developed faith. My mother obviously believed, but we never really spoke much about Christianity in the family.

I simply stopped going to Sunday School when my parents split up. I suppose my mother wasn't in a frame of mind to encourage me, and there was no car to get me there on a Sunday morning. So Sundays became what they are for most people; a day of looking after one's own affairs, lying in, watching TV or whatever. Church and God featured very little in my life.

Is there anybody out there?

I do remember starting to pray when I was about twelve years old. The reason was simple: boys' grammar school, lots of exams (yours truly hating exams), all mixed with a lack of self-confidence. What was the outcome? A cry for help to someone, or something beyond myself. It's amazing how many people say they pray when they're in trouble!

Anyway, I found myself sort of praying, usually last thing before going off to sleep. It was really talking in my head along the lines of 'If there's a God out there, please will you help me with my exams.' It wasn't exactly faith-filled, nor did I know if there really was a God out there. I was actually just hedging my bets. I suppose that made me an agnostic; someone who doesn't *not* believe in God, but who simply isn't sure if there is a God. Funny that it seemed natural to call for help. Was that just because of insecurity? More of that later.

The point is I had no concept of being able to have a relationship with God, if he existed. 'He' was just an amorphous, distant concept somewhere outside, way beyond me. That's how I left it for quite a while; I didn't really challenge God and he didn't appear to challenge me.

The early 1970s was an interesting time spiritually speaking. We'd lived through the 1960s with the Beatles experimenting with eastern spirituality. Christianity had largely been seen by the younger generation as belonging to the establishment.

At best it was boring, at worst it supported everything that was corrupt. Certainly it was increasingly irrelevant to many people.

By the time I reached sixth form most of my contemporaries showed no interest in Christianity. We had traditional school assembly every morning with a hymn and Bible reading before the Headmaster's notices. I remember there was an unofficial sixth form choir. Half a dozen lads in the sixth form balcony would belt out the hymn as loudly as they could and suddenly stop singing halfway through. The lack of singing amongst the rest of the boys would become immediately obvious, while the Headmaster found himself virtually singing solo. It wasn't the best advertisement for Christian worship. It also didn't help that we'd all had to read the Bible compulsorily at some stage in our religious education at school. Christianity had become just one more thing to poke fun at as part of the 'great rebellion' amongst teenagers!

In all of this there were seeds of a renewal of interest in Christianity amongst young people. Across the Atlantic the so-called Jesus Revolution was capturing people's imaginations. Young people who had been caught up in the hippy culture of the late '60s were finding that only Jesus Christ could really satisfy them, rather than drugs or free sex. It probably didn't hit Britain in quite the same way, but we always watch what goes on in the United States with interest. Meanwhile, many churches in this country were experiencing a renewed experience of God's power – the 'charismatic renewal' movement as some called it.

Of course, I was completely ignorant of all this, but I did have a friend at school who was claiming he had been 'born again' and insisted on talking about this person Jesus. I had never really thought about the person of Jesus seriously before. I knew the stories about him. I had been to Sunday School when I was little after all. The figure of Christ was probably more prominent in our culture when I was young. I'd had to read the Gospels in 'Scripture' lessons, but the Bible wasn't very real to me, it was just an historical book full of stories that probably weren't true.

Meanwhile, my involvement with that youth club was to lead me along a path I hadn't bargained for. The leader of the club happened to be a member of the Baptist church where the club was held. He kept on to me about going to church. Now I hadn't set foot in that church for a number of years. I wasn't a religious person. I preferred listening to the Beatles, or to Simon and Garfunkel and other pop and folk music rather than hymns and religious singing. I didn't know one end of a prayer book from the other. I wouldn't know how to behave in church. No way was I going to start going. But he was persistent, this bloke. Eventually, just to get him off my back, I turned up in my best clothes one Sunday evening.

How strange it was. It may have been a Baptist church but it was relatively ornate and certainly very 'church-like'. I remember sitting there thinking 'now does this make me a Christian because I'm sitting in this place again?' The answer was that it didn't make me a Christian any more than going and sitting in my mother's garage would have meant I was a motor car. I knew deep down that this was not a natural place for me to be.

There could only be one reason I carried on going – something, or someone, was drawing me. I couldn't explain it. I suppose I probably would have stopped going were it not for the fact that the same youth club leader persuaded me to go along to a 'fellowship group' of young people at his house after church on a Sunday evening. Now imagine what that meant for a shy retiring type like me – slight panic actually. How could I relate to a bunch of teenagers sitting round drinking coffee (that's where I learned to drink the stuff) and talking about things? I was incredibly nervous, but I became hooked on listening to other people's conversations. I mostly sat and listened without uttering a word.

What sort of things? Well, I can't remember everything but I do recall they talked about issues that had never really bothered me before. The threat of nuclear war and the end of the world was a good one. In those days we still lived in the shadow of the Cold War and people still talked about the four-minute warning. Just what could you do in four minutes anyway? Then there was the whole issue of the meaning of life; what were we here for if we were just some sort of high form of animal and everything stopped when we died?

Some people claim that Christianity is all about escapism. It's to do with retreating from the cares and issues of the world and finding comfort in some sort of pie-in-the-sky-when-you-die faith. For me, the process was the exact opposite. I'd spent most of my life up to that point rather wrapped up in myself and my own cares and plans; cares that could cripple me socially and plans that may never see the light of day but were still all about my own world, even those high ideals of Welsh Nationalism. These new subjects were forcing me to think way beyond myself, about the whole past, present and future of the human race in fact. Maybe I was an intense sixteen year-old, I don't know. All I do know is that I didn't particularly *want* to think about such things.

Beginnings

There were probably three things that happened to change my life at that point. The first was one short moment when the youth leader's eyes fixed on me and he asked, 'And what does Anthony think?' I remember going bright red and stuttering some sort of opinion on whatever the subject was. That wasn't fair of course! As anyone who has ever done an *Alpha* course knows, one of the rules is a group leader must never pounce on the quietest person in the room and elicit an opinion. You can say nothing if you want.

So why did I have to say anything? Of course the answer is I didn't, but there were all these faces looking at me expecting something to come from my lips. The fact is the next time they were talking about something I managed to say a few words again. It built up from there. Nothing too complicated about that, I was learning to interact naturally. All the same, I have to be grateful to Peter for that, as well as to Mary his wife for opening up their home.

We can never underestimate those who influence us along our journey in life. I'm sure most Christians can name someone who featured prominently at some point or another. For me, these two were the first of many. That leads me to mention the second life-changing thing. It was when Peter led a session on life after death. He spoke quite simply about his job. Now I have to explain the situation here. Peter happened to be the superintendent of the local cemetery and crematorium. We met in his house, which was actually all on its own next to the roadway going into the cemetery. It was a sort of lodge house, situated behind the large iron gates of the cemetery. The setting couldn't have been more appropriate for talking about life after death!

I have to say I'm not easily spooked, and it didn't scare me at all meeting where we did. However, hearing someone talk who dealt with the dead, quite literally, was fascinating. It really did get me thinking about what happens when our mortal bodies finally pack in. It seems to me that most people spend their lives not thinking about death. If they did, they'd be more inclined to do something about their eternal destiny.

Those that do think about death might come to a conclusion that satisfies them. Perhaps they see their purpose in life as bettering the human race, or merely at the other end of the scale enjoying things while they can; a kind of 'eat, drink and be merry for tomorrow we die' mentality. At any rate neither of these two extremes satisfied me. I couldn't believe that a human being could live a life where deep relationships are formed, where emotions are felt, where perhaps great things are achieved, and yet at the end of it all that's it – the end, nothing. There had to be more. There had to be a purpose and perhaps the possibility of existence beyond this mere physical world.

Now some people might argue that this is simply an expression of insecurity. From how I've described my life so far someone might say it's obvious that I needed a prop in the idea of a better life after death. Indeed, perhaps believing in a God who gives that life after death comes from the insecurity of not having an earthly father around. Well, I can't prove anything either way on that score. I can only say that I've met many people over the years who have been insecure and believed in God. I've equally met many people who are insecure and *not* believed in God. What's more, I've met plenty of people who believe in God and yet naturally have every reason to be secure in life!

Actually there was a lot more to it for me than just an emotional response. After all I did have a brain. There were lots of questions going through my mind as I said earlier. At my school there were others who were 'searching'. While some were merely into discovering the adult world through booze, sex, drugs and rock 'n' roll, others were exploring the spiritual realm. A lad I knew was into Scientology, then a relatively new phenomenon. Someone else was a Jehovah's Witness, arguing vehemently with anyone who called themselves a Christian that Jesus Christ couldn't possibly be divine. As it happens, that was quite an issue for me as I began to think things through concerning Christianity.

Discovery

The third thing that happened to change things for me was my discovery of the Bible, and with it a fascination with the person of Jesus Christ. I mentioned earlier that we were actually made to read the Bible in lessons at school. For me it was very much a closed book, something I had heard stories from when I was little. Although I guess it was part of my culture, I'd never actually read it for myself.

In our group on Sunday evenings we started to look at the Gospel stories. As I heard about this amazing person Jesus I began to realise that there was much more to him than I had ever thought about. It wasn't just the fact that these writers of the Gospels talked about miracles he performed; it was much more the character of the man and the things he said and claimed about himself. What was it that drew people to him, to the extent that they would simply leave their livelihoods behind? How could a simple carpenter's son speak with such authority, apparently know people's thoughts, confound clever religious leaders, so profoundly change the lives of people he met?

My knowledge of world religions was limited. Nevertheless I knew of no one else who began such a great movement as Christianity by allowing himself to be killed. Why did Jesus tell people that he was going to be crucified, that that was in fact why he had come? Did he really come back from the dead? All these were questions that I'd never considered before, but now they began to burn in my brain.

I decided the only way I could really get my head around all this was actually to read the Bible myself. I asked for a Bible as a Christmas present and duly had one in a modern English translation. I began to read it. However, I'm one of those impatient people who can't wait to find out what happens in a story, especially if it's a long one. So rather than starting at the beginning and ploughing my way through it I went straight to the last book, the Book of Revelation. Nobody told me that wasn't the best place to start!

Actually, I'm rather glad I did start there because what I received in reading that was a powerful sense of the majesty and greatness of God. I didn't understand much of what I read since it's a book full of imagery and prophecy about the end of the world which many people have tried to interpret over the years. All that aside, I gained a strong sense of the fact that God is in control of human history and will bring all things to a successful completion when Jesus returns to bring judgement and justice to us all. This Jesus that I had become fascinated with wasn't just a carpenter's son; he wasn't the 'gentle Jesus meek and mild' that I remembered from childhood; he was the risen, ascended, glorified all-powerful ruler of the universe. He was the object of worship by the saints, the angels and all the creatures of creation.

This picture of Jesus was significant for me at that time. I've mentioned that one of the people I knew at school was a Jehovah's Witness. He presented a very convincing argument about Jesus being the Son of God, created by God but not actually divine himself. To someone such as me who didn't know the Bible very well this was very confusing, as the message I was getting from Christians was the opposite. I read some of the Jehovah's Witness literature and bits of it seemed to make sense. It was particularly interesting to read about their views on the Second Coming of Christ, since there I was reading about it in the Book of Revelation.

Nowadays I don't find it too difficult arguing from Scripture that Jesus is divine, our God who became one of us. Back then I didn't possess that knowledge, but I had a very simplistic way of looking at it. There I was reaching out, searching to know the truth about God and seeking to find him if he was indeed there. That being the case, I wanted to go straight to the top. I wasn't interested in any 'middle man'. Call that arrogance if you want but I wanted to know the top man for myself!

'Come in!'

I mentioned earlier that I had begun praying because of exams. Without going into all the arguments about what prayer actually is, quite simply for me it was an attempt to communicate with God. In my mind and sometimes out loud I was using words. Although it was on a very simple level of 'help me!' there was actually something much deeper going on; without realising it I was inviting him to come closer, indeed to become a part of my life. Gradually, he was becoming much less of an abstract idea of love, power or whatever. He was becoming a reality, indeed a real person.

Some could argue that this was merely a psychological process. As I said earlier I was very aware that I could be looking for some sort of abstract father figure, some sort of prop or comfort than I needed because of my insecurities, or maybe even just a strong person to look to for inspiration and guidance. However, I would argue that the process was more than just emotional; it was a mixture of that and an intellectual desire to understand the truth. At the same time as developing in prayer I was seeking to find answers, particularly to understand whether there might be a purpose to my existence.

There were many things I found hard about what the Bible said, particularly what Jesus himself taught. He spoke about following him whatever the cost, about 'taking up your cross'. He spoke about persecution for those that follow him. He spoke about putting him above everything and everyone, including your own family. He spoke about the idea that sin is not just what you do outwardly, it's about the very state of your heart. Above all, he spoke about judgement upon sinners who refuse to repent. He spoke quite openly about the existence of Hell.

That last one was particularly difficult. Put quite bluntly it meant that if I decided to follow him and put my trust in what he did for me on the cross my salvation would be assured; but those that didn't follow him, including members of my own family, did not share that same assurance, so they were not assured of an inheritance in heaven, rather the opposite.

Now it seems to me that someone who is looking for comfort in a faith system is hardly likely to choose the kind I'm describing. Yet that's what I did in the end. I have to say it was something I discovered without a lot of outside encouragement. Much is said these days about how the journey to faith is different to what it used to be. People now need much more to belong to a church group before they'll believe, and before their lives will change. We see this process happening a lot; it's particularly pronounced amongst young people for whom belonging to a peer group where they're loved and accepted is important. Although they still need challenging, many become Christians as they see the reality of faith in those around them; the natural thing is to become a part of what they see.

Of course I was part of a small group. I was becoming accepted within the church I'd started going to. However, I must explain that at that time this particular church was what one would describe as quite 'liberal' in the kind of theology that was taught there. The youth leader himself bucked the trend to a degree, but generally within the church the whole notion of God's judgement was not talked about. I would argue therefore that the main basis for what I believed in terms of needing to come to Christ for forgiveness came from what I read personally in the Bible, rather than from the views of peers.

In the Book of Revelation there's a very well-known verse where the Lord Jesus speaks directly to a church:

> 'Here I am! I stand at the door and knock. If anyone hears my voice and opens the door, I will come in and eat with him, and he with me'. (Revelation 3:20)

Although the Lord is addressing the church in that verse, it's often been used by evangelists to describe what needs to be done for somebody to become a Christian. Indeed, over the years I've used it that way myself many times. However, in my months of searching and reading nobody explained to me actually how to become a Christian. I'd read that verse without really relating to it personally.

I mentioned that I had a friend at school who himself had become a Christian. He was a Scottish lad who happened to be quite big and good at rugby. His size was important, bearing in mind that I wasn't that big and he was a useful friend to have around! One Saturday he invited me over to his church where for the first time I did hear an evangelist talk about asking Jesus into your life. The verse he quoted, of course, was Revelation 3:20.

That night I went home, got on my knees next to my bed and prayed. I said, 'Lord, I think you've been coming into my life over the last few months but just to make sure – *please will you come in.*' I guess it's true that he had been coming in over a period of time, but there's nothing like speaking, out loud, specific words of invitation like that. In the end he knows exactly when I became his child, but I'll put it down to that date. I'll always remember the date because earlier that day I'd watched international rugby on TV with my friend and his father at their house. Wales scored a memorable victory over Scotland by one point in the dying minutes at Murrayfield thanks to a kick by John Taylor. It was 6th February 1971 and I was a lot happier than my friend and his dad that afternoon!

Difference

So what difference did that make? Well, as I said earlier there were probably no enormous things outwardly that people would notice straight away. What I noticed, though, was that my prayer life became different. No longer was I praying to somebody 'out there'. Instead, Jesus was very real. I knew that he had come into my life. Also, I no longer seemed to have any doubts about the afterlife. Oh, I didn't know what heaven would be like, but I knew that if it was going to be with the Lord Jesus forever it was going to be good! The main thing was that thanks to this new relationship, thanks to what Christ had done for me on the cross, my eternal destiny was now in him. I knew I was going to live forever.

I think most people who become Christians would say that God challenges them at some point in their lives to make choices. The very act of responding to his words 'follow me' involves choice, deciding to take a different path to the one you might have been on up to that point in your life. But there may be other issues to be dealt with afterwards, depending on what that original path had been like. Sometimes it means giving something up. That might be because the 'something' is obviously sinful; it might have been a habit, an action or an attitude that the Bible specifically says is wrong. However, it might be that God simply wants to ask who is Lord of your life. Are you prepared to follow him on his terms, not your own?

For me, there was a choice to be made. I felt very strongly that I was being called to follow someone who was saying, 'Follow me come what may; give everything to me'. There was to be no fence-sitting; either I was in the kingdom of this world and doing things the way I wanted to, or I was in the Kingdom of God where he ruled and what he said was law. It seems to me that too many people want to have a Saviour, but are not prepared to follow a Lord. As far as we know, the first ever Christian creed was not 'Jesus is Saviour' but 'Jesus is Lord'.

Now a lord two thousand years ago was someone who had absolute rule in his sphere of influence. You didn't question his word or command. I began to learn not to question the Lord Jesus. And it became clear fairly soon that he was asking something of me. Previously I've mentioned my being a member of the Welsh Nationalist Party. In terms of what I actually did at that age it didn't mean an awful lot; in terms of what I dreamt of, of where my energies were directed, it meant a great deal. Quite simply, I felt God saying it was time to lay all that down. So I did. It's not that there's anything wrong with Welsh nationalism, nor that I can't be proud to be half Welsh. For me, I was being called to channel all my energies into becoming a disciple of Jesus Christ.

Of course, at that stage I had no idea I would end up ordained one day. Nor did I have any inkling about how much God would have to do deep within me and how painful and difficult that would be.

CHAPTER FOUR

GROWING WITH THE HOLY SPIRIT
Who makes me me? 2

'Holy Spirit *what?*'

Later on in 1971 I heard about a big rally that was going to take place in London organised by The Nationwide Festival of Light. It was all to do with making a stand for morality in Britain. I was up for most things in those days and thought it would be a good experience to join several thousand Christians rallying in Trafalgar Square and Hyde Park. It seemed I was the only one from our church who wanted to go, but a friend of mine found a place on a coach with another church group.

It turned out to be quite a day. There were lots of interesting speakers and colourful banners proclaiming things like 'Jesus Is Alive' and 'Moral Pollution Needs a Solution'! The march to Hyde Park was interesting. It was the first time I encountered a movement called the Gay Liberation Front, which had been founded only the previous year. It was all about homosexual people showing the world that they weren't afraid to admit their sexuality and that they were quite happy or 'gay'. It was an example of a rather nice word being somewhat hijacked by a pressure group. Anyway, all I really remember is lots of people dressed rather outrageously, seeing the odd smoke bomb and smelling the odd stink bomb thrown at the Christians as exception was taken to what we were marching about.

The evening rally in Hyde Park was exciting, particularly for me as a young Christian. It was great hearing the American evangelist Arthur Blessitt for the first time. However, the real significance of the day turned out to be the journey home. Unbeknown to me I had been booked in with a coach full of Elim Pentecostals. Now I knew nothing at all about the Pentecostal Church, but I was soon to learn. They were a very friendly bunch, keen to know about me and how I became a Christian. They asked me if I had been 'baptised in the Holy Spirit'. I wasn't sure what they were talking about and they did their best to explain in the time allowed on the coach home. One of them recommended a book to me called *They Speak with Other Tongues*[1] by a man called John Sherrill. I promised to read it.

Now being part of Baptist Church meant I already had a particular understanding of baptism. I knew it was to do with expressing your faith outwardly and publicly. It was an act of commitment, not to be undertaken lightly but after serious consideration. Partly I think because I wasn't really challenged by anybody, and partly because of lack of confidence, I didn't get baptised until March of the following year. Nevertheless, I knew it was going to be a hugely important step that I was going to have to take.

In the Baptist Church baptism usually means being completely immersed in water. Part of the imagery in such an act is the idea of dying to your old self as you go under the water and then rising to a new life in Christ. It was also the means of becoming a full member of a local church. So I was fully versed in the whole idea of *water* baptism. However, 'baptism in the Spirit' wasn't actually a phrase that I had thought very much about.

More

John the Baptist said of Jesus 'I baptise you with water, but he will baptise you with the Holy Spirit.' (Mark 1:8). Theologians have argued over the years about what it means to be baptised in the Spirit. Many say it's to do with what happens when you become a Christian. If Jesus comes into your life, then he does so by means of his Spirit. He sets his seal upon you as a child of God by his Spirit. It's therefore tied up both with your entering the Kingdom of God and with your baptism in water, whether the latter be as a confessing believer or as a child (as in other church traditions).

We can argue about words and phrases until the cows come home, but what really counts for me is what makes a difference in my life and whether I'm brought closer to God. The phrase 'baptism in the Spirit' was being used increasingly in Christian circles back in the '70s (and by Pentecostals before that) to describe an experience of receiving the Holy Spirit in a much fuller way than he is received at conversion. Since then, mostly to avoid theological arguments, people have preferred to use other phrases such as simply 'filled with the Spirit' or 'released in the Spirit'.

As it happens, the idea of being baptised in the Spirit wasn't that complicated to me. I was captivated by what I read in John Sherrill's book. Here was a clear-headed investigation by a journalist into the phenomenon of speaking in tongues. To cut a long story short, the conclusion of the book was that this was indeed a gift from God that first occurred on the Day of Pentecost as recorded in Acts chapter two. It was mentioned several times after that and has occurred throughout history, along with a host of other supernatural gifts given to the church. As I read the book I became more and more aware that I wanted this particular gift to help me in my own prayer and worship life.

I wanted other gifts too, such as prophecy and healing, so I could be more effective in telling other people about Jesus and sharing within the church. Why shouldn't I? After all, the Bible says we should earnestly desire spiritual gifts (1 Corinthians 14:1). I could find nothing that told me these gifts died out at any point. To me it was obvious that the church needed supernatural power these days as much as ever in order to win an

unbelieving world for Christ. But this gift of tongues in particular fascinated me.

I knew that when I prayed and tried to reach out to God in
worship I was severely restricted. I knew the usual phrases in
English to worship, such as 'praise you, Lord', 'you're wonderful', 'I love you, Lord'. I could, of course, sing hymns and
worship songs, read aloud the Psalms, but nothing seemed
adequate to lift my spirit into the heavenly realms. There was
something in me that wanted to go closer to him in worship,
deeper in spiritual experience, but somehow my own human
limitations prevented this. Another way of putting this is that
it was like having him standing in the hallway of my house
when I wanted him to come into every room. Yet another
picture I had in mind was of a gas boiler with just the pilot light
burning when what was needed was all the burners to be at
full blast!

In fact, the very word 'baptism' gave me my ultimate way of
thinking about this. Originally the word was used among the
Greeks to signify the dyeing of a garment by dipping. It became
a word used by the Jews to do with ritually washing one's self
really well. It had something to do with the idea of being
drenched. Plato used it metaphorically of being overwhelmed
with questions. John the Baptist apparently needed 'plenty of
water' to baptise people (John 3:23). As a Baptist my experience
of baptisms was to see people overwhelmed by a lot of water
as they were immersed fully, not a mere sprinkling as on the
head of a baby. So, that was it: I wanted to be overwhelmed by
a lot of the Holy Spirit not just experience a little wetting!

'Hands-on' experience

It was clear to me from reading the experiences of the first
Christians recorded in the Bible that the normal experience
was for people to lay hands on those who were to receive the
Holy Spirit. It didn't say it had to be by specially ordained
people. I asked a couple of friends if they'd do this for me and

they did. As far as I could tell, nothing happened. It was really disappointing. I was expecting some sort of feeling to well up within me, sentences to form in my mind that I could then perhaps speak out. I didn't give up and some time later I had another go. Same thing – nothing! Was this really something God wanted everybody to have? Maybe I'd misread the Scriptures.

It wasn't until some time later that I was to realise how this actually works. By this time I had become involved with a thing called Youthquake at the cathedral in Birmingham. These were fortnightly Saturday evening meetings that had begun under the leadership of David MacInnes, the Precentor of the cathedral, and led by Nick Cuthbert. I was really grateful for these meetings. About six hundred young people would pack the place, worshipping in a lively way and enjoying the excellent teaching from David, Nick and others. Not only were they a great way of meeting other young Christians from across the city and from different church traditions, but they were the first time I had had consistent and regular Bible-based teaching, including much about the Holy Spirit.

One evening I was helping clear up afterwards. We were in the vestry of the Cathedral and I asked Nick to pray with me.

I said, 'Nick, I've tried to clear out all the sin in my life. I've done everything I can to concentrate on Jesus and still I haven't received the baptism in the Holy Spirit.'

His reply was pretty straightforward: 'You can't earn what God wants to give you as a gift. You need to ask him, believe he's given you that gift, then thank him and go on doing so.'

Nick and someone else laid hands on me and prayed for me to be filled with the Holy Spirit. Nothing happened, or so I thought.

'Now go home, keep thanking the Lord that he has filled you with his Holy Spirit and see what happens,' were the instructions.

So that's what I did. All the way on the top of a double-decker bus; all the way from the bus stop to my house; all the way to my bedroom. I was determined that I wasn't going to let go of this. I lay on my bed and decided I would do nothing but concentrate on Jesus, worshipping him with all my mental energy. I spoke out loud using all those phrases that I could think of. I decided to repeat the word 'Hallelujah' a few times. It was the only non-English (Hebrew) word I knew!

Suddenly, as I was praising a word or part of a word popped into my mind. I can't remember what it was, but my first thought was that I was making it up. However, determined as I was I decided I'd speak it out loud. I immediately felt silly. Surely this was simply the power of the mind? After all, I'd been seeking this gift for a long time. Never mind, I persisted and spoke the word or part-word out again. As I did, more words came, then more as I spoke.

I can only describe what I felt as a sort of warm glow spreading throughout my entire body, rather like being immersed in a bath of warm water or even having a mild electric current passing through me. The most important thing, however, was that I felt the presence of the Lord Jesus in that room and in me in a way more real than I ever had before. My brother, who was not yet a Christian at the time, came up to my room and wanted to know to whom on earth I was talking!

It was twenty past midnight on a July night in 1972. I'd been a Christian for seventeen months. In the Bible people usually seemed to get filled with the Spirit pretty much as soon as they became Christians. I'm really grateful that the delay for me wasn't any longer. It was in any case the result of being thoroughly convinced of the rightness and naturalness of the phenomenon. I hadn't become prejudiced against it as many people are for a variety of reasons. What I did learn very clearly is that when God gives you something you have to step out and use it. He may only give you the first little bit; perhaps a syllable to be spoken out if it's tongues; perhaps only a phrase if it's prophecy. It does involve an act of the will, a co-operating with him and not just waiting for something to 'come over us'. For me, the words came *as* I spoke them, not before.

So what?

Well that was my experience anyway. I remember the next day feeling really flat because I didn't wake up feeling any different. I couldn't hear any words in my mind that weren't English. I wanted to tell people about my experience and indeed I did, with mixed reaction. Some wanted the experience as well, others I think thought I was a bit off the wall. I remember David MacInnes being thrilled to hear about it, and then reminding me that sometimes the Spirit moves in us like a shallow, bubbling stream making a lot of noise but to be truly filled with the Spirit he also needs to move in us like a slow, deep river as he does his work in us. It's hard to forget wise words.

The thing is, what if everything I've described was simply self-indulgence? What if it was all just for me, to make me feel good about God and about myself? There are several things I want to say about that. The first is that I had a clear understanding about spiritual gifts as they are recorded in more than one place in the New Testament. They are given primarily not to individuals but to the community of the Church. They're not toys to play with but tools to use in the building up of that community. Even the gift of tongues could be used in this way, both prophetically and in intercessory prayer as well as in one's personal devotional life. Moreover, gifts of the Spirit were given so that the Church could witness and evangelise in supernatural power.

It wasn't long before others in my youth group were receiving various gifts of the Spirit, particularly prophetic words. Sunday evenings became rather interesting. After the service in church we would assemble in one of the rooms in the church hall and carry on worshipping and waiting on God to distribute his gifts and speak to us as he chose. They were very exciting times, although I think the church leadership struggled to understand what was going on.

The second thing to say is that although my experience was both spiritual and involved the emotions, it was far from being emotionalism. It wasn't just about having good feelings about the Lord being close. I had to learn to use the gift given to me. I've used tongues pretty well every day in the years since, and still they build me up and release something indescribable within me. However, I'm always in control of them, by which I mean I can shut off at any time. Often there is no particular emotion involved. I use them to worship and to pray about situations when I basically don't know how to pray. I use them in praying with others to receive something from God. Occasionally I use them in situations where authority needs to be taken over the demonic.

Now I would never say to anyone that in order to be filled with the Spirit they must speak in tongues. There is no scriptural basis for saying that, and I recognise that we're all different. The only thing I can say is that I don't know how I would get by in my spiritual life without the gift of tongues.

The third thing about all this is perhaps the most relevant to what I'm trying to say in this book. I don't think I realised at the time quite what being filled with the Spirit meant. Those words about the deep river would prove so true. True renewal in the Holy Spirit isn't just about receiving gifts, nor even having power to serve God better. It's really about opening yourself up completely to what he might want to do in you. It's a process that lasts a lifetime. He is the great Master Surgeon.

The lamp of the LORD searches the spirit of a man; it searches out his inmost being. (Proverbs 20:27)

We often think such a verse is talking about God knowing our thoughts, God judging us perhaps. But when he 'searches' us he's not just looking for things with which to find fault; I believe he is searching us to pinpoint and deal with the things that need healing and putting right. Hebrews 4:12 says something similar:

For the word of God is living and active. Sharper than any double-edged sword, it penetrates even to dividing soul and spirit.

I was to discover in the coming years that being renewed in the Spirit is actually a very painful experience if you're serious about letting him do his work. As Patrick Dixon says:

> Living faith that leaves us emotionally untouched is a faith in the mind only, a mental assent process that has failed to touch the depths of our being.[2]

Opportunities

While all these things were going on in my spiritual life, I still had various things to come to terms with, particularly with what I was going to do with my life. A recurring theme in this book is lack of confidence. Sharing in bringing up my own children has made me realise how much gets passed on and how much I missed having a father around.

As I say, my mother never married again. Despite never really getting over the divorce she was nevertheless a very resilient woman. She went back to work as a teacher, managed to buy my father's half of the house, and had quite a reasonable social life. When I was sixteen she was involved in a very nasty head-on car crash when the driver of the other vehicle fell asleep at the wheel. She recovered fairly well, bought a more robust car and got on with life. When she was fifty-nine she was diagnosed with breast cancer. She went through many traumatic bouts of treatment, as the cancer spread to her oesophagus, bones and lungs.

I witnessed my mother's faith in Christ growing during this time. She moved back to Wales for the last two years of her life and, despite her frailty, was out having her hair done the day before she died. Obviously when she died at the age of sixty-seven it was like losing two parents at the same time, but despite her strengths and our undying gratitude for what she gave us she could never be a father as well to my brother and me.

It's hardly surprising therefore that there should be issues of confidence on my part. During the period when I became a Christian, I began singing and playing my guitar in front of people. The first time I ever did it was to a few people at school. I shook so much goodness knows how I managed even to hold the guitar let alone play it. The next time I had a go it wasn't quite so bad, the next time slightly better, and so on. Eventually I found I was really enjoying being up front. Who knows, I thought, maybe I could take this up as a career. Some years before that I'd fancied being an actor, so maybe deep down there was actually a showman trying to get out!

Coupled with generally becoming more socially capable, my shyness became far more manageable. I truly believe that there was a healing work of God going on within me. The beginning of performing in front of people coincided with my spiritual journey. I soon found that I wanted to sing and write songs about Jesus, and that's what began to happen. At that time there were opportunities in Christian coffee bars around the Midlands. I would sing and simply speak about Jesus and what he meant to me. Opportunities arose to accompany one or two speakers in other situations such as school missions.

There were also opportunities to perform in a place called The Jesus Centre in the city centre of Birmingham. This was an old building converted into a café and teaching facilities. It attracted young people from all over the Midlands and became a great resource to local churches. There were many events including concerts by established Christian artistes, with people like me doing the odd floor spot.

Could it be that this was what God was calling me to? When I became a Christian I knew I was entering 'ministry' because all Christians are called to minister the Gospel and the power of God in this world. I firmly believe that all believers are priests in the biblical sense of the word. There is a calling on all of us who follow Christ to play our part, it just so happens that some people are ordained to work full-time in church leadership or whatever. However, I did wonder from very early on whether I might be working full-time for God as well.

'I'm nearly famous now'

As proved to be the case later on, there was indeed a calling to full-time Christian work. Looking back, however, it's obvious that the Lord had a lot more work to do in me before that was to happen. At the age of twenty-one I did go to my minister to enquire about training for ordination in the Baptist Church, but although he was enthusiastic I got cold feet, feeling I was just too young. I had only just been made their youngest ever deacon, and I suppose I was still hoping that there might be opportunities in the music world. I probably should have been more realistic about my talents.

It's been said that everybody has his or her 'fifteen minutes of fame'. One of my favourite personal stories is how Cliff Richard was once my warm-up act! In 1973 he was in Birmingham making a film called *Take Me High*. An opportunity arose at the same time for some Christians to go into Swinfen Hall prison near Lichfield and talk about their faith. I was asked to join in but I couldn't make it to the first evening. However, Cliff was available and kindly agreed to take his guitar in and perform to the inmates in the prison chapel. Apparently many of the lads there thought it was a wind-up that Cliff Richard was coming, so not too many turned up. Well the next week they didn't have Cliff; instead, they had me singing. Because of the previous week lots of them turned up. It did my ego a lot of good. The problem was, the *next* time hardly anybody came!

My only other claim to fame in the Christian music world is to have performed on the main stage at the very first Greenbelt Festival in 1974. To cut a long story short, if you sent in a tape of your songs and they thought you were any good you got a slot. It was the main stage because that was the only one there was. I got to perform on the first afternoon to what looked like a tiny number of people way below me scattered about this field in Suffolk. It was a bizarre experience. A few years after that I actually made a cassette of some of my songs and took it to sell at

Greenbelt. This time I only got to perform on the 'fringe'. I sold a total of two tapes all weekend. So who else can say they started on the main stage and worked their way down like that?

In all seriousness it was quite an issue for me early on. I just didn't have the self-belief to go and train for something after my school years. I struggled to complete those in the end and didn't feel I had the confidence to go away to university. Instead I started working for the Department of Health and Social Security, in what was then called Supplementary Benefits. It was the 'end of the line' for many in a way, government financial assistance claimed when everything else proved insufficient or non-existent. At the age of nineteen I was out visiting people in their own homes. Many homes were very nice, but equally many were some of the poorest in the country. I saw a variety of people, often in long-term poverty or recently fallen on hard times. It was an education.

Water in the glass

So that was it. I had been full of hope to be doing something glamorous for Jesus, but instead I was in a job I really hated. It wasn't a badly paid job, effectively junior management in fact. But the red tape and the aggravation that went with every day just got me down. Had God forgotten me? Certainly, I remember the first day I started visiting. I had no car at first. Three bus rides had taken me to a rundown outer city housing estate full of high-rise flats and blocks of maisonettes, each floor of which seemed to be guarded by a vicious Alsatian dog. Nothing could have prepared me for working in that environment. Yet I'm sure God was testing me, both in terms of being patient and in terms of sorting out many of my feelings.

The feelings I'm talking about I suppose were disappointment, feeling passed by, but above all envy of those who seem to have been chosen by God for more interesting things like preaching or singing full-time. Having worked now for a number of years in full-time Christian ministry I know the realities of it. But the grass is always greener on the other side. . . .

Actually, I'm not sure that I always really understood *what* I was feeling at the time and that was the nub of the problem. I'll return to the whole question of understanding feelings later on, but for now I just want to emphasise one very important thing. No matter what I felt I was going through, it wasn't all bad. I knew deep down that the Lord had his hand upon me and there was a plan for my life. I went through periods of melancholy but thankfully they didn't last too long. With the help and encouragement of friends I would manage to emerge from them and carry on with life.

The real crunch in terms of God's challenge to me of the need for healing was yet to come. I had still to learn the true meaning of being renewed in the Holy Spirit. Sometimes when Christian speakers talk about being filled with the Spirit they use the analogy of a glass being filled with water. In one sense this is not a bad picture, especially if the water overflows, since we're meant to 'overflow' with the Spirit into the world. The problem is that we can end up seeing the Spirit and the vessel as separate. There's us and there's God, who graciously comes into our lives, like the picture I used before of coming into the house. But it's not merely that, it's about *relationship*; the Spirit and my spirit coming into a new bond.

The Bible says that when two people get married they become one flesh, they become in a sense one person. In fact it's more than that. When two people are in a good marriage relationship the 'person' they are is more than simply the sum of two individuals. Essentially, that's what it's like with God and me. There's not just me, filled with him; there's a whole new me. That me is different to what it was, throughout every aspect, from the cells in my body that will one day be perfect at the Resurrection to the depths of my spirit and my emotions. And as the Spirit does his work everything about me will be impacted.

Notes

1. John L. Sherrill, *They Speak With Other Tongues*, (Baker Book House Co., orig. publ. 1964).
2. Dr Patrick Dixon, *Signs of Revival*, (Kingsway Publications, 1994, p. 240).

CHAPTER FIVE

UNDERSTANDING AS THE BEGINNING OF HEALING

Why change?

> Three things make people want to change. One is that they hurt suf-
> ficiently. They have beaten their heads against the same wall so
> long that they decide they have had enough. . . . They want to
> change.
>
> Another thing that makes people want to change is a slow type
> of despair called ennui or boredom.
>
> A third thing that makes people want to change is the sudden
> discovery that they can.[1]

By the time I came to apply to university I really thought my
life was coming together. I'd shaken off many of the feelings of
being left out, jealousy or whatever. There was a new hope of
getting out of the rut of the job that I didn't feel suited for. There
was obviously a new excitement at being accepted onto a good
course. My confidence was riding high. God was really in
control.

I decided not to leave home to go to university. I don't *think*
it was because I was tied to my mother's apron strings,
although I know I was concerned about leaving her on her
own (my brother had been away to university and by now had
left home permanently). Admirable though a sense of responsibility is, it can't be right if it prevents someone from spreading their wings and taking the normal course of leaving home.

The main reason was because being four years older my life as a young adult in Birmingham was more established. I had a wide circle of friends, mainly through all the Christian contacts I had. In all honesty, I knew which side my bread was buttered on as well. Living at home without overheads, having my meals cooked for me *and* getting a student grant was pretty good.

I often wonder how things would have turned out if I'd had the courage to go to university straight from school. Probably I'd have been forced to be much more independent. As it happens the Lord obviously had plans to sort me out, in more ways than one. I shan't go into all the details, but within a fairly short space of time I changed from being a civil servant to a student (with quite long hair). I'd fallen in love with a girl from my youth group and together we had begun attending another church, St John's Harborne. There were various reasons for this, but as it happens St John's was much closer to where we were to live when we eventually got married.

As far as I knew, no one in my family nor Jane's had any dealings with the Church of England. St. John's was not how I thought of a typical Anglican set-up. It had lively services, believed in the gifts of the Holy Spirit and had a thriving work amongst students and young people. Eventually we were to join a home group, get married there, and be very much part of the church community. From the beginning of our relationship Jane and I had had a feeling that God wanted to use us together in some sort of ministry. We had no idea that this would eventually mean my being ordained in the Anglican Church.

All this change was against the backdrop of the events described in Chapter One. I've already described the feelings I was experiencing by now. They were to do with feeling left out, perhaps unimportant, this time however much more intensely than ever before because the 'other person' was far closer than anyone had been to me before. It was, quite simply, painful. The feelings were incredibly intense, and yet I had difficulty identifying exactly what they were. The important thing is that

I knew I wanted to change. In the words of Thomas Harris, I 'hurt sufficiently'.

It's possible!

I'd venture to suggest that most people who suffer to any degree with psychological difficulties want to change. That is of course unless they are the sort of people who enjoy the attention of the church minister, the doctor or the psychotherapist. There are those who can end up playing mind games and in the end don't really want to change. Remember, Jesus still often asked sick people what it was they wanted. However, I know from talking to GP friends that many people in our doctors surgeries are there because their illness has psychological origins, be it stress, depression or whatever. One presumes that even those hoping for a quick fix medication want things to be different.

For many it may not be always as intense as it was for me. They may have learned to live with their ambiguous feelings yet they know deep down that things aren't right. They may not feel out-and-out despair but there might be a continually gnawing weariness with it all. Finally they just might get around to doing something about it. My experience, however, is that it often needs somebody or something to come along and challenge them.

The idea that it is possible to be different isn't always obvious, but when people are faced with it they can either run away or decide to do something about it. Thomas Harris speaks about people being exposed in some way to the ideas of Transactional Analysis and realising that change is possible. Exponents of other kinds of therapy might argue the same for those methods. The whole basis of Christianity is that things definitely can be different! I knew this to be true in my own life. Things had changed. I *was* different; I had more purpose than I did earlier in my life. I did find joy in my relationship with the Lord Jesus. I did believe there was a purpose in my life. But now it was time to up the ante.

The Bible has a lot to say about change. It talks about the need for it almost from the beginning. Because humankind decided to go its own way and not God's there was what is known as the Fall. Rather than arguing about the ins and outs of this as a one-off event it's probably more helpful to think of it in terms of the ongoing consequences, where we see human nature as essentially self-seeking. There is the tendency to put all sorts of other gods before the Lord of creation (the first of the Ten Commandments is, 'You shall have no other gods before me'). So most of the Bible is about God's long-term plan to restore the relationship with him that our self-seeking, our sin, has spoiled.

Everything throughout the Bible points to the cross, where Jesus performed the great act of sacrifice to pay the price for our sin. Putting our faith in that act and in his risen Son makes the believer 'born-again', a child of God. Salvation is assured, our status is definite. But there's much more to it than just booking your ticket to heaven. Dr Martyn Lloyd-Jones puts it like this:

> . . . The Kingdom of God is not like that which you have always known, it is something quite new and different. The first thing we have to realise is that 'if any man be in Christ he is a new creature (he is a new creation), all things are passed away, behold all things are become new.' If only we realised as we should, that we are in a realm in which everything is different! The whole foundation is different, it has nothing to do with the principle of the old life.[2]

There is now something to aim at, not just a hope for the future but for a new life now. In quoting the Apostle Paul (2 Corinthians 5:17) Lloyd-Jones is reminding us that this is about something far greater than just bettering yourself, dealing with a few emotions or whatever. This is about complete change into becoming a new person.

This is where we could get into a lot of theological language. We could use a word like 'regeneration', meaning that being born-again is both about a one-off entering into a relationship with Christ, and an ongoing process of being changed into the child you're meant to be. Others will speak about 'sanctification', the process of being literally 'made holy'. This is nothing to do with gaining a halo and walking around with a sort of hazy smile on your face! The word 'holy' literally means 'different' or 'set apart'. Yes, when you become a follower of Christ you are indeed set apart from the world, even if you are still called to live and work in it. However, sanctification is the story of what happens for the rest of your life here on earth. It's about changing and about allowing him to do the work of change in you.

Real change

There are those who say that once you've become a Christian you should be able to rest in the victory that Christ has won on the cross. Your life should continually reflect that victory, and there should be no place for sin or sickness. However, anyone who is being honest will tell you that the Christian life is never that easy. In fact, many people will say that their troubles only really began when they became Christians! That's because they entered into a spiritual battle and the battle with themselves that may not have been so real before.

One of the most helpful Bible passages for me in thinking about this is 2 Corinthians 3:16–18:

> But whenever anyone turns to the Lord, the veil is taken away. Now the Lord is the Spirit, and where the Spirit of the Lord is, there is freedom. And we, who with unveiled faces all reflect the Lord's glory, are being transformed into his likeness with ever-increasing glory, which comes from the Lord, who is the Spirit.

Yes, the veil has been taken away (the original Greek for 'unveiled faces' literally means *'having been* unveiled'). This means things are no longer as they were in the Old Testament, where only someone like Moses could approach God. His face shone as a result, but he wore a veil because others were frightened to come near him. There was literally a barrier between them and the presence and glory of God. The veil was also a picture of people being blinded to the truth. Now, however, the veil has been taken away and believers can come near to God. Our faces are 'unveiled' and as his children we have the right to enter his presence.

But the story doesn't stop there. Paul says we are 'being transformed into his likeness with ever-increasing glory'. Here the 'being transformed' in Paul's original Greek is indeed the present tense. It's quite clear he's talking about an ongoing work in us. And what is that work? To be changed into his very image; that is to become like him. Many Christians understand that perfectly, but largely they see it in terms of character or behaviour, of showing the fruit of the Spirit in their lives – love, joy, peace, patience, kindness, goodness, faithfulness, gentleness, self-control, and so on. This indeed is holiness, to be right and godly in the way we behave.

But even that's not the full story. I believe that to become like Christ isn't just about behaviour, it's about attitude and state of mind. It's about being at peace in your heart, which means being comfortable with yourself, the world and your Heavenly Father. It's about being in touch with your feelings and not ruled by them. It's about having self-confidence, without becoming overbearing. Jesus himself displayed all of these characteristics, even in the relatively short human biographical glimpse of him we get in the Gospels.

Jesus of Nazareth was humble yet strong in character. He got angry at what he saw was wrong, but he didn't throw tantrums. He never allowed himself to be manipulated, nor did he manipulate others. He was not frightened by the religious leaders who held outward power in society, rather he was completely secure in the knowledge that he was accepted by his heavenly Father, who was 'well pleased' with him. That's how he could teach with such authority and not be afraid to speak out against injustice and hypocrisy.

That's how I want to be

Well that's how I wanted to be – like Jesus. As I said previously, I thought that any difficulties or ambiguities in my feelings could simply be boxed up and laid on one side. Mostly, I had been growing in the faith, so I thought. My Bible knowledge and prayer life weren't too bad. I wrote and sang songs about Jesus, I could even tell people about him fairly comfortably. What I had yet to face up to was that change, in the language of the Holy Spirit, was much more than just behaviour. Allowing the Holy Spirit to have full sway in my life, truly to renew me, meant opening up some of the darker cupboards that I had kept closed for many years. Indeed, the cupboard doors needed to be removed and never replaced!

I think the truth is that even if change in the Christian life were simply to do with moral behaviour, many Christians couldn't move on in that anyway because of so many hindrances within them. These can be of many kinds; spiritual, social or emotional in origin. Anyone who is serious about moving on with God knows how hard it can be. Even Paul talks about his struggle; he says that so often he knows what is the right thing for him to do but his sinful nature within him prevents him from doing it. No amount of positive thinking seems to help him:

> What a wretched man I am! Who will rescue me from this body of death? Thanks be to God – through Jesus Christ our Lord!
> So then, I myself in my mind am a slave to God's law, but in the sinful nature a slave to the law of sin. (Romans 7:24–25)

There lies the key of course. Ultimately only the power of the Holy Spirit can change us. We don't have the strength in ourselves to reach our full potential as children of God. The good news is that he always wants to give good things to his children. Jesus said the good Father will give the Holy Spirit to those who ask him. As I said previously, though, we have to know what we're asking for. Jesus responded not only to people's needs, but also to those needs expressed in request and faith. What a problem it is if we have needs that involve our emotions, but we can't even identify what those emotions are.

When I first had therapy I simply didn't know what it was I was feeling. I certainly couldn't give it a name. I must admit I didn't know what to expect. I was sort of hoping that somebody would give me all the answers; they'd identify my problem and the feelings associated with it and tell me what to do. Maybe they could even hypnotise me or something, and I'd be OK afterwards. Actually, I have serious reservations about such a method, but what I'm really trying to say is that I wanted someone else to do the work. What I didn't appreciate was that the answer had to come from within *me*. This is how non-directive counselling works:

> . . . the healing that comes through psychoanalysis and psychotherapy invariably comes from within the patient – stimulated by the questions of the psychoanalyst or psychotherapist of course, but still from within the patient.[3]

Why should this be? I've often heard people say, 'God helps those who help themselves'. That's actually rubbish. You won't find it anywhere in the Bible, rather you'll see hundreds of instances where God helps those who *can't* help themselves. The whole notion of his dealing with sin and sickness is based on his grace and mercy. Grace is something we can't earn or create. It doesn't mean that he hasn't given us the ability to discover means of enabling healing; otherwise we might as well not bother with medical science. But I really believe that ultimately all healing, physical or emotional, comes from him. That's why my story is that God has healed me.

However, in the whole area of emotional healing *understanding* is a very important concept. I don't mean that we have to understand everything intellectually, but we do need to be able to identify feelings even if we don't know exactly how they came to be there.

Understanding is power

'The light shines in the darkness, but the darkness has not understood it'. (John 1:5).

These words at the beginning of John's Gospel are well known and profound. However, for a long time I found it hard to grasp what John was really saying. The first Bible I ever owned and read was the New English Bible translation, which says of the light, 'the darkness has never mastered it'. My second Bible was the Revised Standard Version which says, 'the darkness has not overcome it'. Now I didn't have any problems with that. It seemed quite straightforward to me; John is talking about the great battle between light and darkness, between good and evil, Jesus shining as the light with the devil and all that is evil never being able to overcome him. Simple!

Then I bought a New International Version (NIV) of the Bible, where the verse reads as above. But surely that's different! Overcoming something with power and understanding something are two different concepts aren't they? I thought I'd better check it out, so I had a look at the old Authorised Version. Well that didn't help, because it said 'the darkness comprehended it not', which is really the same as the NIV. What exactly was John saying if that was the right translation?

In fact the original words that John uses can mean both – 'to seize, to win, to apprehend, to lay hold of' *or* 'to find, to understand'. Some people think that this choice of words was deliberate on John's part and that his contemporary readers would indeed see both meanings. But it still doesn't explain the implications of the darkness not *understanding* the light. Then I thought about what understanding really is. Understanding gives you power, at least to an extent. John's word actually combines the two, in a sense.

We can think of examples of understanding and power. For thousands of years disease and sickness had complete power over human beings. People were at the mercy of nature taking its course. But when they began to understand more about the workings of the human body, about bacteria and viruses, they could begin to look for cures. We almost take understanding in the field of medicine for granted, and there's much yet to discover of course, but the fact is knowledge and understanding always come before the cure.

As I'm writing there's a thunderstorm going on outside, a fairly rare event for where I live. Time was when thunder and lightning held people in complete fear. They didn't understand what was going on and would perhaps interpret the occurrence as the wrath of the gods or God. We will never tame nature, but at least understanding things such as what causes lightning or other weather phenomena gives us some degree of control over our environment.

In the Imperial War Museum in London there's a whole section devoted to special military operations and how intelligence has been gathered over the years. On the wall is a quote by Field Marshal Earl Alexander, who commanded the 15th Army Group in North Africa in the Second World War: 'Without an efficient intelligence organisation a commander is largely blind and deaf.' Alexander obviously appreciated the value of discovering as much as you can about your enemy, his strengths and weaknesses, his intentions. You also need to understand how the enemy thinks, what motivates him, what he might be afraid of. History is littered with the mistakes of armies that have gone into conflict situations without really understanding what they're up against.

The darkness has never understood the light. The devil *cannot* understand God; therefore he will never overcome him. If we understood God we would be on a par with him. I think there's something of this idea in the story of Adam and Eve in Genesis 3. There is the whole idea of disobedience of course, as the couple ate the forbidden fruit. Perhaps the tree of the knowledge of good and evil is something to do with gaining a godlike understanding, or indeed a degree of understanding God. Of course this would never actually be possible, but the couple are tested in how much they trust this God they'll never understand and sadly they fail.

And so once again to feelings. If we don't understand our feelings they will always have a degree of power over us. They might even dominate our lives if they're strong enough. To be able to recognise them, to *name* them, is important. When Jesus met a demonised man (Mark 5) he ordered the evil spirit out of him. The man shouted a question and a request, but rather than entering into a dialogue Jesus simply asked him his name. He replied 'Legion,' because he had many demons. In his compassion for the man and demonstrating his total authority Jesus cast out the entire lot, enough to possess then a large herd of pigs. Naming the demons seemed to be part of the process of exorcism in this instance. We don't know how often Jesus did this, but in this particular case the man's confession of the name seemed to help in his being freed. What's important is that Jesus had some understanding of the demons and not the other way around.

I'm not advocating a particular strategy for deliverance ministry. Nor am I meaning to imply that emotional difficulties have their origins in the demonic. Occasionally they may do, but more often they don't. Nevertheless, the parallel point I'm trying to make is that to identify or name an emotion will rob it of much of its power and, I believe, enable the healing process to begin.

In the mirror darkly

The problem for so many people is that they find it hard to identify their feelings, or if they begin to they might then suppress them out of fear for what those feelings might do to them. The irony is that the feelings are already causing them problems. In the eighteen months that I saw someone on a weekly basis I was at times very frustrated. I realised after a while that it was no good trying to intellectualise my situation. I wanted to appear very level-headed, but at the same time I knew I was often talking round in circles. What I really needed to do was express the feelings more rather than try to describe them in a sort of detached way.

Well I'm not sure how successful I was in the end. As I said before, I was certainly able to identify feelings of being left out of situations and a degree of suppressed anger with them. To an extent I could relate them to the time when my parents split up. It was all really to do with the lack of self-worth, of feeling deep down that I was not significant or important. I therefore needed things to happen in life that would make me feel important. When that didn't happen I could just get a sort of low-grade depression, but basically I lived with it, as there was enough in life to counter the effects. I'm happy to say getting married was a beacon of joy in all that! The real problem was when I perceived something happening to make someone else important, particularly of course Jane, as she was the one closest to me. Putting it bluntly, the feeling was an angry jealousy or envy; it's just that for some reason I hadn't been able to identify it. I want to say more about jealousy in a later chapter.

Maybe if I'd been able to let my anger really rip in a therapy session the feeling would have been clearer to me. As it was, it was a slow process and at the end of my eighteen months I was only beginning to see, rather as in a mirror darkly (1 Corinthians 13:12). I think probably it was more that the therapy gave me the tools to continue looking at my feelings without allowing them to dominate. They didn't need to be a source of fear, but neither should I have seen them as things to be boxed up in my mind. They were part of who I was as a whole, yet I could face them as an adult.

I left university with a decent degree in English. Now began quite a test of how comfortable I was with myself as I found myself unemployed. During my degree I really enjoyed a creative writing course and wanted to use that in some way. I started to apply for copywriting jobs in advertising companies. Journalism would have been perhaps another alternative. However, being well established in Birmingham I didn't really want to move to London where it would be easier to get jobs, nor was I particularly enamoured with the thought of further study and training. Over a period of several months I applied to the fifty or so advertising companies in the West Midlands. I had a grand total of one interview and they appointed someone else who had experience.

Unemployment seemed at the time fairly degrading, especially having worked on the other side of the benefits system. It's quite hard to keep a sense of purpose while you're writing off for jobs and getting lots of rejections. I did work for a few weeks for our landlord, clearing the enormous garden of an old Victorian house. It was very satisfying getting rid of the huge amount of undergrowth and trees. A whole flight of steps appeared that nobody knew was there. I suppose it was something of a picture of what God was doing in my life, clearing out the overgrown stuff and revealing what was underneath.

At the time there was something of a recession going on, which is why I found it difficult getting work of any description. Either I didn't have the experience or training, or people told me I was too well qualified because of my degree. I couldn't win! Eventually I got a job working for the City Council. It was a clerical job, well below the level I'd been working at in the Civil Service, working out the wages of school dinner ladies. After a few weeks I managed a bit of a promotion within the Council and started working in a careers office, trying to organise the office and helping young school leavers to find work.

I firmly believe that when your life is given over to the Lord Jesus you can rest in the knowledge that he has a plan for you. Looking back, I would never say that my experiences have been a waste of time. Even being unemployed and working in jobs that I found less than fulfilling have given me valuable insight into other people's lives. Not only that, but often the more difficult periods in my life have turned out to be times of character development, even though at the time I might not have seen the point! They've forced me to rely for my ultimate fulfilment on my relationship with Christ and not on circumstances. What's more, the period following university could easily have finished me off, given what I said about issues of self-importance and so on. I suppose the fact that I came through it all relatively unscathed is proof that there had been a measure of healing in me.

Calling

Anyway here I was, several years on from leaving school and still not settled in a particular career. Certainly I'd managed to lay down the whole idea of doing anything full-time with music. I began to wonder why God wasn't leading me towards a career, perhaps in teaching or something if it wasn't going to be writing. I had become good friends with the curate at our church, actually doing some singing with him on occasions. He suggested that maybe the Lord was leading me towards ordained leadership. At first I couldn't believe that would be true. I'd always thought vicars came from a certain stable; usually public-school with a very academic background. In the past I thought they were all old, wore half-rimmed glasses and always spoke in a parsonic way.

Having spent the last twenty-plus years trying to counter people's preconceived ideas about vicars, it's hard to believe I thought that way too! Certainly, St John's Harborne dispelled the myth. I had a much better idea of the Bible-preaching, vibrant side of the Church of England with a leadership that had vision and energy. Maybe it wasn't so far-fetched that I could be part of that leadership. I must admit, I knew very little about the Church of England and the whole prospect was very scary. That's not the point, though, since what's really important is listening to God and to what he's calling you to do. Jane and I obviously prayed and talked about it at length. We both felt it might be what God wanted and I went to talk to the Vicar, Tom Walker, who was very supportive from the outset.

The selection process for ordination training meant seeing several people before ever getting to a selection conference. I wondered how much I would have to say about my past. It had been some time now since therapy. As it happens, the issue didn't arise at first because the Director of Ordinands for the Diocese felt I needed to have a period of a couple of years before he was prepared to take things any further. The official reason was that I hadn't been confirmed very long as an Anglican, but I think it was probably also to do with the fact that it hadn't been that long since I was unemployed. Anyway, I had to wait another two years, working in a clerical job I didn't find easy. More patience required, not to mention more testing of the emotions.

Meanwhile, Jane and I were asked to lead a new venture at St John's. There was a real need for somewhere for single people in their twenties and thirties connected with the church to meet and just enjoy being together as an alternative to the pubs or clubs. Every Saturday night Jane and I led this in a converted barn. There was a small amount of spiritual input plus of course all the 'pastoral extras' that went with that kind of ministry. It was a big commitment, but excellent preparation for what was to come in our lives.

Notes

1. Thomas Harris, *I'm OK – You're OK*, (Arrow Books, orig. publ. 1967, p. 58).
2. D.M. Lloyd-Jones, *Spiritual Depression*, (Pickering and Inglis, 1965, p. 128).
3. Dr John Lockley, *A Practical Workbook for the Depressed Christian*, (Authentic Lifestyle, 1991, p. 336).

CHAPTER SIX

PERSONAL MAKE-UP
What makes me me? 1

What a piece of work is a man! how noble in reason!
how infinite in faculty! in form and moving how
express and admirable! in action how like an angel!
in apprehension how like a god! the beauty of the
world! the paragon of animals!

(Hamlet, Act II Scene II)

So complicated

Stand in front of a mirror for a few minutes and look at yourself.
Say to yourself, 'What a remarkable person I am!' Some people
don't have a problem doing that because they're naturally vain;
others will just feel guilty or maybe not like what they see. The
truth is, every single one of us is truly amazing. The Psalmist
says, 'I praise you because I am fearfully and wonderfully
made' (Psalm 139:14). Indeed, every single human being is a
miracle of creation. God knew us even before we were born,
and the natural thing should be to praise him for what he has
created.

But have you ever actually stopped to think about how complicated you really are? You are the product of an amazing
array of processes, some going back to before you were born,
others that have happened since. Indeed, the human race is so
complicated that it will probably never fully understand itself.

Medical science has made tremendous advances, but there are still diseases and conditions to conquer. Historians and sociologists are continually reassessing society and social movements. As for the human brain, there always seems to be something new to learn about it, and experts go on disagreeing about how it works.

Even just before starting this chapter I've learned something new from the newspaper. Apparently research has found that children whose ring fingers are much longer than their index fingers are more likely to be hyperactive and bullying. It seems the effect, due to testosterone exposure in the womb, is particularly pronounced in boys. Children with long index fingers, by contrast, are more likely to be neurotic and sensitive. A quick look at my hands shows my ring fingers are certainly longer than my index fingers, but I don't remember being hyperactive and I certainly don't think I was ever a bully. The trouble is, when you read things like that you're tempted to have a surreptitious look at other people and make rather sweeping judgements about them!

More seriously, the very same newspaper quoted the Archbishop of Canterbury on the eve of a study by the Children's Society, investigating how a lack of family care in the UK appeared to be the biggest cause of spiralling childhood distress. Rowan Williams spoke of a new generation of 'infant adults' who have been deprived of a caring childhood and have grown up to become violent and dysfunctional:

> The pincer movement of the commercialisation of childhood and fragmentation of the family is now closing. We are talking about ingrained unhappiness among large numbers of children. There are high levels of clinical depression. If you think of cultures that tried to do away with the family in the past you will find they did not survive.[1]

It's pretty worrying stuff, and it all adds to the complications of living in this world and developing as human beings. If you actually think of all the different things that contribute to make us the people we are, it's a wonder most of us make it through life at all! What I'd like to do over the next few chapters is change gear slightly and think about some of the things that shape us. It's not an exhaustive list, simply some of the things that I have come across in my own life and ministry that seem important.

As I have said, this is not meant to be a textbook and if any of the areas I look at are particularly relevant to you or interest you, I would urge you to explore more expert sources. What I hope to do is include how particular factors have been pertinent to me in my journey of self-understanding. I don't particularly endorse any single one to concentrate on as the answer to everything. As with many therapies and viewpoints there will be good and bad in them and I believe we're called to use our brains to discriminate, to take what's useful and leave the rest. It's important to remember that we are the result of many paths joining up at the place we're at now. None of them stands alone and we must look at the whole picture, remembering that we won't always be absolutely sure how it came to be.

Genetic disposition

From the physical to the mental

This is probably the one I, like most of the population, am least qualified to talk about. Yet I do think many of us are aware of such matters we hear about in the news from time to time. We know there are physical conditions inherited genetically. The whole field of genetics has opened up vast amounts of knowledge to us along with the possibilities of cures beyond what previous generations could have imagined. As with all gifts from God (and I take the ability to discover as a gift) we can use or misuse them. Here isn't the place to explore the whole question of medical ethics, but we do need to pray that we learn to use our knowledge in the right way.

My concern is to consider how many of the things that go to make up my personality, emotions, desires and moods have been genetically inherited from my forebears. That is to say, how much of me is down to those thread-like structures found in the nucleus of all cells (except red blood cells) which contain my genetic material or DNA? The answer in part of course is that I'll probably never know. Scientists are a long way from providing all the answers and I doubt they'll all come in my lifetime. There is so much yet to discover.

We do know that some mental attributes, just like physical ones, have a tendency to appear in relatives of those suffering from a particular condition. For example genetic studies using various techniques have shown relatives of people with schizophrenia are more likely to show signs of schizophrenia themselves. We know that such things can apparently skip a generation. Sometimes this is because the specific combination of genes wasn't evident in the middle generation. Instead they lie dormant only to be passed on to re-emerge a generation later. Whether they will or not seems to be simply a matter of statistics. Only rarely, when both parents have the same gene do the odds get stacked in favour of one chance or the other.

Studies will always tend to concentrate on the more extreme forms of mental problem, but even then they won't agree. For instance, bipolarism (formerly called manic depression) seems to occur in families but there could be many causes of it even though some studies concentrate on genetic reasons. I have no doubt at all that we should rejoice in what has been discovered and pray for the development of the right treatments in extreme cases. But what about the whole host of less extreme conditions that may or may not be down to our DNA? The final answer, I believe, is that no matter what is discovered in the future each one of us is still unique in the eyes of God. His desire is that we should be whole people, healed and restored to a full relationship with him. Even if some of the way I am as a person has been genetically influenced, the Holy Spirit can still break in and bring healing.

It's important to note that I'm still talking about a *physical* cause of something. I want to talk later about sin and its consequences through the generations, curses, family taboos, and so on, but these are not my concerns here. It is of course helpful if you're able to trace some of your family history. The problem there is that many things won't be recorded even if you can go back a few generations. All I can say about myself is that there are things to rejoice about and things to keep an eye on. I'd say there are certain musical loves and abilities, for example, that have been passed on through my mother's family. Her father taught himself to play the piano and various other instruments, such was his natural ear. Apparently he played the piano in the silent movies. Of course it's interesting that music and singing should be a particular national characteristic, in this case of the Welsh. Both Jane and I love music, so it's no surprise that our children have followed suit.

My mother was quite a strong character and I'd like to think I've inherited some of her characteristics, perhaps in being able to stick to a cause or keep going when the going gets tough. Inevitably I've asked myself what I've inherited from my father. Not his artistic ability, that's for sure. It looks like a tendency to high blood pressure, but not his ability to tan well in the sun! More seriously, I've asked questions about his tendency to a kind of moroseness. Quite how bad this was I'm not sure. In more recent years, before he died, he spent much time on his own. Sometimes he would phone up and we would speak for quite a long time, while he was obviously struggling with his loneliness and becoming quite melancholic.

Not easy to evaluate

I'd better explain briefly about the contact my brother and I had with our father. After he left we would see him on Saturdays, though not every week. After a while, my brother and I found this too much emotionally and we asked that we stop doing so for a while. He moved to various addresses, eventually having another family. It meant that contact with him slowly became reduced to cards and presents from him at birthdays and Christmas.

When I was at theological college in Bristol Jane and I lived not far away from him and we renewed the contact. We went to see Dad with his family, and had him and his wife over for a meal. We didn't talk too much about the past but I do remember telling him that I forgave him for leaving us all those years before. In all honesty I did mean it, but at the same time the relationship could never be as it was when I was a child. To all intents and purposes he had not been a father to me for a long time and it was no good pretending that we could just carry on where we left off, even though I could call him 'Dad'.

I can't remember how it happened, but my mother found out that we had renewed the contact and sadly she didn't cope with it at all well. If I had really needed to see my father I wouldn't have let my mother prevent me. As it happened, we moved back to Birmingham for my curacy and I felt we should be very careful how we kept the contact going. In practice, it meant phone conversations; and over the years these tended to be very much 'one way', with him telling me about his life and problems rather than listening very much to things I might have wanted to share. It wasn't really like speaking with a father. You can imagine it wasn't particularly easy.

Anyway, the bottom line is that like many people it's hard for me to evaluate my own parents' characteristics. Was my dad's melancholy due to the fact he was on his own anyway? He ended up being divorced from his second wife. The circumstances were different and of course I only ever heard it from his point of view. Subsequent information has put another slant on things, but the fact is I will always have to keep an open mind. Loneliness is a real problem in our society for a variety of reasons such as the decline of extended families. I know my mother was lonely too, but she was more gregarious than my father, which I'm sure made a difference. In fact my father had dementia in the latter part of his life, as did his mother. Was that genetic? Or was it that neither of them had enough social interaction to stimulate their brains? In any case, both reached a reasonable age.

For me, the important thing was to bring this in prayer to the Lord. Quite apart from any underlying causes of unhappiness stemming from life experiences, I'm sure I had a tendency to moroseness, to a kind of gloomy outlook that was often inward-looking. Simply recognising this for what it was and seeking healing through the power of the Holy Spirit was a release. Whether or not the cause was genetic I received prayer from others to be healed. The point is, the Healer knows the cause; it was sufficient for me to accept the *possibility* of inheriting something like that.

I find it important to be aware of moods, when tiredness in particular can drag me down. But that's all they are, moods; they need have no power. Sometimes it's simply a case of getting enough rest or alternatively of doing something positive such as a practical activity rather than a mental one, even just going for a walk or doing a job in the house. Ultimately of course I have the great weapon of being able to worship in the Spirit, and that in itself is able to bring a completely different outlook quite quickly, to 'lift the spirits' as we're fond of saying. Sometimes just reading Scripture such as a psalm helps, or maybe listening to worship music (rather like the effect David's playing the harp had on King Saul). My wife and children are very good at pointing out my moods these days – they simply accuse me of being a grumpy old man and quite often they're not far wrong!

Another thing I had prayer for was the fact that my paternal grandfather committed suicide, something I mentioned earlier. Again, it's virtually impossible to evaluate. Did he have an inherited disposition towards suicide or were circumstances the main factor? When I first went to see my GP about my problems she asked me if I had thought about suicide. I said it had crossed my mind briefly. I think I said that without really thinking, possibly in order to convince her I meant business with getting sorted out, but I don't think I would ever have done it.

Christians can commit suicide, however, if the 'balance of their mind is disturbed'. I know some other Christians find that hard to accept; it's part of 'the victorious Christian living' syndrome around in parts of the church. The reality is that it can happen. I was honestly nowhere near that stage. *However*, with my grandfather in mind, I have since had prayer for healing and 'cutting off' from any influence, whether it be physically genetic or a form of family curse. Once again, it's all about opening yourself completely to the Holy Spirit and allowing him to move freely within you as he sees fit.

Personality type

A whole industry has grown around personality typing in the last few years. Many different organisations, from large businesses to churches, have taken the ideas on board in order to help solve organisational problems and relationships. Many businesses use personality type exercises to find out more about job applicants. I'm not going to say too much here about it since there is a wealth of published and online information available.

Probably the two best-known methods are the Enneagram and the Myers-Briggs Type Indicator. The latter has been particularly widely used. There has been some controversy about the possible spiritual roots of both methods, particularly the Enneagram. The latter maps nine distinct personality types in diagrammatic form and shows how these types move when under stress and when flourishing. Various people have claimed links to such things as numerological divination (that is, mystical numbers having meaning that can affect our lives) and the Zodiac. It's hard to tell if these claims are justified, or whether people are just making their favourite 'codes' fit, rather like the vogue of trying to find hidden codes in biblical writings.

My own limited experience is with Myers-Briggs. A number of us from our church have done a workshop, learning a little about it and consequently ourselves. We only really scratched the surface but it was still worth it. I realise that some people go much deeper, but for me it's sufficient to understand myself a little better and realise why some of my colleagues and fellow church members don't behave like me! My overall conclusion is that it's very useful to know something about your personality type and how others may be similar or different. It's not simply about whether somebody is extrovert or introvert, there are all sorts of questions about how people take in information, deal with problems and other people, and so on.

The typing begins with where we prefer to focus our attention and where we get our energy from ('Extroversion', more to do with the external environment, 'introversion', drawn to the inner world). It moves on to ask how we prefer to take in information ('Sensing' to do with real and tangible things, 'intuition' focusing on the big picture, relationships and connections). Then it's about how we make decisions ('Thinking' more analytical and logical, 'feeling' more value-led). Finally, there's how we deal with the outer world ('Judging' being systematic and methodical, 'perceiving' being more spontaneous and energised by last-minute pressures and things being open-ended). These values can be combined in sixteen different ways, each four-letter type being described as a 'dynamic energy system'.

My summaries of the various preferences are hopelessly simplified, and it's important to remember that the words have meanings that are not the same as in everyday life. For example, 'extrovert' doesn't mean someone is loud or talkative, just as 'introvert' doesn't mean they're shy. I came out of the test as extrovert, but that hasn't stopped my having issues of shyness and lack of confidence. Myers-Briggs doesn't really answer questions about how people have become the personality type they are, whether they were born like that or have been formed over the years. It tends to favour the former, since it is based on the theories of Carl G. Jung who believed that people are *innately* different in what they prefer. Incidentally, the link to Jung has made some Christians nervous about Myers-Briggs.

Jung had an interest in Gnosticism, spiritualism and indeed a broad range of spiritualities, including the occult. The question is whether those things in themselves mean that a system derived from his theories is inherently bad[2].

The literature that goes with an initial dip into Myers-Briggs does suggest how behaviour can be altered in relation to other people when you know your personality type. It is after all about energy systems rather than simply static 'boxes' that people fit into. It emphasises that there are no right or wrong types and each individual brings special gifts. It also says quite rightly, 'Type does not explain everything. Human personality is much more complex.'[3] It is just one path that leads to the person I am, albeit I think an important one. Whatever we might think about Jung, or about a system that attempts to describe and explain how personality works rather than a person's *character*, we would be foolish not to take it into account, as long as it doesn't become the be all and end all.

Incidentally, I came out as an ENFJ and I love the short description of its characteristics:

> Warm, empathetic, responsive and responsible. Highly attuned to the emotions, needs and motivations of others. Find potential in everyone, want to help others fulfil their potential. May act as catalysts for individual and group growth. Loyal, responsive to praise and criticism. Sociable, facilitate others in a group, and provide inspiring leadership.[4]

Very flattering, I thought, until I saw that all the other types are described fairly glowingly as well! Well, at least some of it is accurate, I *think*.

Male-female differences

What's inherent?

If I'm not always sure what characteristics in me are inherent, there is at least one I'm glad to say I can be definite about; I am a man! I don't want to discuss gender or sexuality ambiguities (for want of a better word) at length here. We know that some people are born where physical gender characteristics are not one hundred per cent fully male or female, but these are a very small proportion of the population. Also, nobody knows how many people are actually homosexual. Gay activists would have us believe it's quite a high number, but there is no proof. Nor is there proof that people are born homosexual.

Personally, I'm convinced that homosexual tendencies may well be due to family relational issues early in life. One of the best explanations I've read of this is by Robin Skynner in a book that was very popular twenty years ago, *Families and How to Survive Them*[5]. He describes what happens when, for example, a boy fails to 'cross the bridge' to his father's side and his sexuality is affected. This is not a very politically correct view these days, and an English bishop has even been in trouble with the police for daring to suggest that people might be 'healed' of homosexuality. The question in the present social climate is not whether this view is right or wrong but whether people can even be allowed to explore the possibilities of psychological causes and therefore 'healing', without being accused of homophobia. We do not live in easy times over this matter, not least in the Anglican Church.

Anyway, that's enough of that. My assumption is that the majority of the population are quite happy with their maleness or femaleness. The problem for most of us is how the two relate to each other, and why things can often go so wrong between them. I suppose it's fairly obvious why this should interest me in particular. Coming from a broken home, the whole subject of divorce and family break-up has concerned me for many years. Being happily married since 1978 doesn't mean I'm ever immune from having problems and I want to understand myself and my spouse as well as I can so that we stay as happy as the day we got married. Some people quote statistics that show children from broken homes have a higher chance of becoming divorced themselves. Maybe in my case it's a question of working harder at things because I don't want history to repeat itself, or maybe it's actually the difference Jesus makes.

The learning process never ends, and too many people seem to forget that some things have to be worked at continually. The commitment of marriage is the arena in which that marriage is worked out; it's not about just staying together while you feel in love or it's convenient. As Bonhoeffer said, 'It is not your love that sustains the marriage, but from now on, the marriage that sustains your love.'[6]

I've obviously been involved with marriage in a professional capacity as well. I always tell couples I'm preparing for marriage that I'm not an expert, but at least we can think together about a few things before they tie the knot. There is of course a host of factors: the family background, financial pressures, whether they've been living together already, children, life changes. But it seems to me the biggest thing that people need to think about is that men and women are very different. Of course this is true for non-Christians and Christians alike. Sadly, Christians are not immune from the danger of marriage break-up, despite what I've said about Jesus making the difference, and despite perhaps their having a higher view of what commitment should be all about.

Vive la différence!

In 1993 John Gray published a book called *Men Are from Mars, Women Are from Venus*. It was a huge bestseller. Lots of people I know have read it; the question is, how many of us remember what it says when we need to? I must admit, when I read it I kept thinking, 'Oh yes, of course, it's obvious.' I wonder how many others like me have wished they could have made millions by stating the obvious! The basic premise of the book is that men and women are *so* different that they might as well come from different planets. Men speak Martian, women speak Venusian; they deal with problems differently, communicate differently and feel differently. The problem is when they don't realise these differences:

> Without the awareness that we are supposed to be different, men and women are at odds with each other. We usually become angry or frustrated with the opposite sex because we have forgotten this important truth. We expect the opposite sex to be more like ourselves. We desire them to 'want what we want' and 'feel the way we feel.'[7]

The more you keep your eyes open the more you see these differences in operation, both in yourself and in others. For example, take the way we deal with problems. As a man, I seem to have a much more 'compartmentalised' brain than my wife. It's also more focused on dealing with things one at a time. So, if there's a particular problem with a person or relationship at church and it can't be dealt with straight away, I'll put it to one side in my mind until the time I think it can be sorted out. Jane, on the other hand, because she's a woman, doesn't compartmentalise in the same way. She will mull over the problem and want to talk it through, until the solution is found.

So who is right? The answer is, both. Sometimes I think my way of dealing with things is how my brain stops itself going into overload. According to the experts, my male brain is wired for linear, sequential thought, and basically I can only do one thing at a time. Women are more able to multitask, because their brains are much more 'open plan'. Often Jane's way is the right one, especially if a pastoral situation needs sorting out more quickly than I'm ready for it to be.

We have a choice in this situation; either we both get frustrated by each other's different approaches, or we compromise and try to remember how the other one operates. She needs to give me space, but I need to listen. Easier said than done, of course. I don't think we're particularly uncommon in this; it certainly seems to fit in with John Gray's observations.

Similarly, if there's something really bothering me I'll do the 'caveman thing'. I'll retreat to the back of the cave and work things through in my own mind. I think I probably do this a little less than I used to, but the trait is still there. According to Gray, the man's retreating gives out the wrong signals to the woman. Because she deals with problems by talking about them, she assumes there's something wrong with the man or that she's done something wrong. She'll approach him and try to talk, but that will only push him further to the back of the cave. She'll think even worse, and so the cycle goes on. No wonder there is a breakdown in communication in so many man-woman relationships!

Another example Gray cites is how information is passed from women to men. Apparently most men aren't very subtle; we need to hear direct questions and explicit instructions. For example, if a woman says, 'the bin is full,' the man hears it as, 'the bin is full.' Actually, what she meant was, 'please would you empty the bin?' I've tried to improve in this department, but it's not always easy. I suppose it's all about not taking each other for granted, trying to hear each other properly and seeing to each other's needs.

Needs of men and women

We are born with needs. Food, warmth, love, touch are all things a baby needs to develop properly. As we grow up our needs become more sophisticated, although underneath we haven't lost what we needed as infants. When it comes to talking specifically about the needs of men and women, we see the Martian/Venusian idea quite starkly.

One of the best books about this that I've read is *His Needs, Her Needs* by Willard F. Harley.[8] Harley was many years a marriage guidance counsellor in the United States. His prognosis for marriage in that country is not good, with very many marriages either breaking up or having at least one partner in an affair. The situation in the United Kingdom isn't much better.

Although the divorce rate in the UK has come down recently, this could well be because fewer people have got married, so those that are may be more committed to the institution. It doesn't mean there aren't many marriages in trouble, or at least where couples are unhappy.

In his years as a counsellor, Harley began to see that most marriage breakdowns were the results of needs not being met. He believes there are five basic needs in a marriage that most men tend to have. There are also five basic needs that most women tend to have. And guess what? They're not the same! It's impossible to say that everybody fits the categories, and when I've used these with couples in marriage preparation sessions there's often been someone who hasn't related to them all. However, it is quite amazing how many men and women recognise the list. It's also quite amazing how many haven't known the needs of their partner.

Often I've been in discussion with groups at church, perhaps socially, and the subject has come round to men and women and our various frustrations. I love throwing into the conversation the two lists. People sit on the edge of their seats, extremely curious to know the 'answers'. Below are Harley's two lists (words in brackets are mine).

The man's five most basic needs in marriage tend to be:

1. Sexual fulfilment
2. Recreational companionship (she's interested in his particular pursuits)
3. An attractive spouse
4. Domestic support (she likes to keep a tidy house)
5. Admiration

. . . And the woman's five most basic needs in marriage tend to be:

1. Affection
2. Conversation

3. Honesty and openness
4. Financial support
5. Family commitment (he's a good dad)

We don't have space here to go into all these in detail, but you can see just how different they are. Some people might look at these lists and think they're not fair. Why should she have to keep a tidy house, for example? As it happens, I believe the household tasks should be shared as equally as possible. However, the argument here is not about what's fair or not, it's about the felt need of the man. If he's the one who goes out to work, he likes to come back to a comfortable home. It doesn't preclude the situation where a woman goes out to work, and Harley admits he's generalising.

Then there's the need for an attractive spouse. It so happens that the visual tends to be more important to men than to women. It doesn't absolve men of the responsibility to keep themselves in reasonable shape, it's just that physical attractiveness tends to be more important to men. Not all women will agree. Similarly, some women might feel that sexual fulfilment is a need they have. However, Harley has observed that most women need warmth, touch and affection more. Even if it is to lead to intercourse these things are important, whereas men are aroused more quickly and are stimulated by sight more easily.

Whether you agree or not with these summary lists, the fact is that generally speaking the needs of men and women *are* different. Problems arise when the needs are not met. Indeed, it might be that only one of the needs is going unfulfilled, but that is enough to create unhappiness and an overwhelming desire to see the need fulfilled. This may lead initially to confiding in someone of the opposite sex. Such friendship that is formed is often a much greater factor in leading to an affair than simple physical attraction.

In touch

So given all these differences, how can anyone get along with a member of the opposite sex? As I've already said, there has to be understanding that leads to compromise. It's not only knowing something about how your partner works though, but about what makes *you* the person you are, as a man or a woman. Have you recognised your needs, how you feel about things, how you react to different situations? I may have had my problems in the past that have forced me into some self examination, but these questions about gender differences are just as important, and indeed they apply to everyone.

What's interested me over the years is seeing time and again how all this operates. I've seen also how often men can get 'left behind'. What do I mean by this? Well, it seems to me that women are much better at recognising their feelings *and* articulating them. You notice that one of women's needs is conversation. Women see the value of conversation for conversation's sake. They will talk and enjoy the very act of talking. I'm not being funny here, nor sexist, because I think this is actually a strength.

Take the telephone for example. If I phone somebody, it's either to impart information or to find something out. Usually, after a couple of pleasantries, I've done my business and say goodbye. Jane, however, will talk much more widely with someone. She will still have sorted the information out, but she'll have found out a lot more as well, not in a nosy way but in a way that enhances the relationship with that person. On the whole, men tend to talk about things – sport, cameras, computers, cars, and so on. Women will talk about relationships, feelings, issues to do with health and wholeness.

If you don't believe me, listen in at the next social gathering you go to. Have a look too at the magazines in any newsagent. Publications aimed at men are about hobbies and *things*. Women's magazines are full of issues to do with improvement of home, health and happiness. They talk about feelings and relationships, and basically how to be a better person.

It's my belief that in the last few years women have developed far more than men. They have grown in confidence, partly as a result of not being necessarily tied to childbirth. They know how to socialise in the fullest sense of the word. They find their worth through relationships. Men, on the other hand, often get their worth through what they do as a job. They tend not to be able to verbalise their feelings; indeed they often don't understand them as well as women understand theirs. Men will trust other men much less than women trust women, because we tend to be more competitive. This may well be something quite natural, but I'm certain it's born also of insecurity.

I realise I'm generalising enormously, but in my job I do have the opportunity to deal with and observe both sexes in ways that many occupations wouldn't allow. Particularly interesting, and in many ways disturbing, is how things can develop when women become Christians. Often, a woman will come to faith much more easily than their spouse (again, not always true but usually). She then finds that she has not only a new faith, but a new confidence in her identity as a child of God. She has new friends, indeed very close brothers and sisters in the Lord. She may join a home group where she finds herself discussing issues of relationship and, bluntly, how to be a better person.

Meanwhile, where's the husband? He doesn't know all these new friends. She seems to be different, much more in touch with her feelings even than before. The whole thing is a threat, and so often there is increased tension which can lead to marriage difficulties, especially when the husband expresses his resentment of the church or the Christian faith. This is hardly an argument for not preaching the Gospel and welcoming all, but it is an important factor for churches to recognise.

What about the men?

So where does that leave us men? In the last few years there have been attempts to redefine what being a man is all about. The so-called 'new man' appeared for a while, but I'm not sure if anyone really knew what that meant. We're still basically confused. We know we shouldn't be defined by what we do for a living. We know that women have certain rights and opportunities they didn't use to have, and quite right too. But what gives us *our* worth? For a Christian, the answer is clear; we all get our worth from being children of God. But does that mean that men have to worship or 'do church' the same way as women? The issue of masculine spirituality is a live one. Are many men put off church because they see it as too feminine? And what about what the Bible says about men's 'headship'?

I'm not going to try to answer all these questions, because there are simply too many of them and the issues would all require several books each. For my purposes here I simply want to underline that being a man or being a woman is important because that's how God made us. We need to recognise our differences, our needs and our weaknesses. As a man, I've often thought that actually I'm a member of the weaker sex when it comes to emotions. This is what Robin Skynner says:

> . . . I'm constantly impressed by how much stronger women appear to be than men. On the surface many of them may seem less confident; but basically they have their feet on the ground much more firmly . . . They're not keeping up acts in the same way, they don't live in dreams of status and power and achievements to the extent that men do. And because they don't take that stuff very seriously, they're not so fragile, their egos aren't so delicate.[9]

Lots of questions there, then, if it's true. If women had been in charge of the world would we have seen so many wars throughout history? Are men naturally this way and always have been? Or have we actually lost what it means to be masculine because, for example, father-son relationships often go wrong? And are they going wrong more these days?

All I can say from my own experience is that I have become much more aware of my needs as a man, mostly because of having to come to terms with the difficulties of my relationship with my father earlier in my life. I do believe that God has broken in and brought healing for me. Because of having to be almost ruthless with myself in thinking about my feelings and allowing the Holy Spirit to deal with them, it's caused me to think more widely about such issues as what makes a man a man, and a woman a woman. Meanwhile, as with so much to do with the human race, the search for answers in this field goes on.

Notes

1. Quoted in The *Sunday Times*, 17th September 2006.
2. See Rev Ed Hird, 'Carl Jung, Neo-Gnosticism, and the MBTI – An Interim Report', ARM Canada (www3.telus.net/st_simons/arm03).
3. Isabel Briggs Myers, *Introduction to Type*, (6th ed., CPP, 1998, p. 42).
4. *Ibid.*, p. 13.
5. Robin Skynner and John Cleese, *Families and How to Survive Them*, (Methuen, 1983, pp. 244–249).
6. Dietrich Bonhoeffer, *A Wedding Sermon from Prison*, May 1943.
7. John Gray, *Men Are from Mars, Women Are from Venus*, (Thorsons, 1993, p. 10).
8. Willard F. Harley, *His Needs, Her Needs: Building an Affair-Proof Marriage*, (Monarch Publications, 1986).
9. Skynner and Cleese, *op. cit.* p. 251.

CHAPTER SEVEN

MY BACKGROUND
What makes me me? 2

No man is an Island, entire of itself; every man is a piece of the Continent, a part of the main; if a clod be washed away by the sea, Europe is the less, as well as if a promontory were, as well as if a manor of thy friends or of thine own were; any man's death diminishes me, because I am involved in Mankind; And therefore never send to know for whom the bell tolls; It tolls for thee.

John Donne, *Meditation XVII*

No one is an island

The last chapter dealt with factors that some might say are out of their control. Certainly they're ones we might call quite fundamental to making us the people we are. On the whole, they are fairly individual-orientated; they're your genes even if you inherited them from someone else, your personality type is yours, and you're a man or you're a woman, and so on.

However, even with these factors we need to remember that nobody exists on their own. None of us has just appeared out of nowhere, beamed to earth like Mr Bean. We *belong* in some sort of family group and in society as a whole. Becoming more self-aware in order to allow ourselves to be renewed by the Holy Spirit means including taking a look at some of the collective factors that may have had an influence on our personality and character.

In looking at these, we are in no way absolved from our indi-vidual responsibilities. It's no good just saying you're a victim of circumstances or of things beyond your control. Yes, there are things that we can't change, especially if they have their origins in the past before we were even conceived, but in becoming more aware of these influences we then need to bring them to the Lord and ask to be set free where necessary. Only in that way will we be able to be a real influence ourselves – on those around us, on our families and on society as a whole.

Indeed, later on I want to explore how inner healing comes in part from being more aware of the world around and of its needs, in a sense being 'centred' on others as a result of being centred on God rather than ourselves. Being involved in a church commu-nity helps here, for indeed when one church member suffers every one suffers, and a true community learns to bear each other's burdens. Being truly open to the Holy Spirit also involves becoming aware of the needs of the wider neighbourhood and society around you. 'Any man's death diminishes me' becomes a reality, especially if you're concerned for people's eternal destiny.

I think it's important, therefore, to be aware of the commu-nal influences on us. We are part of history, and any generation that is unaware of factors that have gone to mould it lives very dangerously. We should learn from the past, but sadly we all know how often that doesn't happen. It doesn't mean we need to be bound by the past. When Jesus Christ breaks into anyone's life he brings a revolution and I believe he has ulti-mate power over any influences upon us. Nevertheless, being more aware of them means we can bring them to him and allow him to be Lord over them, bringing his healing where neces-sary and affirming that which is good.

Where One's From

Movement

'Where are you from?' is a question most of us have probably been asked on many occasions. The answer will depend on a number of things, according to what we see as important. We might be proud of where we were born or we might just want to talk about where we live now, if that's different. Some people struggle to answer, especially if they've moved around quite a bit in their lives, perhaps with a parent's job. We live in an age where travel has never been so extensive. In the western world people are free to choose where they live to an extent never seen before. People now choose to retire to a nice place, maybe even abroad. There are currently great debates in the United Kingdom about 'citizenship'; do people born abroad but who have moved here see themselves primarily as British or not?

For countless millions in the world this is not the case, of course, and people in our society need to remember that many do not have the advantage of choice in where they live. Because of their poverty they have only ever known their particular village or neighbourhood. Those that do move might do so because they feel forced by economic circumstances, or even natural disasters, although it always amazes me how people will doggedly rebuild their homes in the same place after earthquakes, floods or whatever. Maybe they haven't always got choice.

I think it's probably important we remember that people have always been on the move. Even God's very own people, the Israelites, became nomadic for a long time. It was many years before they settled in the Promised Land and generations later they found themselves exiled and on the move again. In the past the British Isles saw great movements of population as Celts, Romans, Saxons and others landed in England and moved westwards, each time subduing or pushing other tribes out or sometimes intermingling with them. In post war Britain there have been great movements again as people have sought to 'escape' to better areas of the country. The present need for more housing, due in part to an increase in smaller family units and single people, will see yet more changes.

What does this do to people's identity? What happens to local pride or a sense of community? Having lived in a more rural

setting I've seen how people from the cities have been desperate to be somewhere where they can 'settle' and find just that
sense of belonging, where people know each other and they can
be proud of their village. Equally, mind you, I witnessed many
people who simply brought with them a city mentality, where
they didn't make the effort to get involved locally and hardly
knew anyone. This was often a profound problem for retired
couples who enjoyed each other's company but had moved
many miles from family and previous support structures. When
one of the couple died, the other would find themselves very cut
off, and the rural idyll did not fulfill their dream after all.

Shaped by where we're from

Having said all this about the movement of peoples, the fact
remains that most of us have things about us that have been
shaped by where we come from, both locally and nationally. In
the past there's been a tendency for Christians to ignore or even
to decry national characteristics. When Christianity first started
spreading, there were two great messages in this respect. Firstly,
being a Christian meant belonging to the Kingdom of God as
well as to your country or the Roman Empire. 'Jesus is Lord'
was the first great Christian creed. He was the one to whom ultimate allegiance was owed, and this of course became a real
issue in a world where Caesar was supposed to be Lord.
Secondly, the great wall that divided Jew from non-Jew had
been broken down by Jesus' death on the cross. It was clear from
the epistles:

> There is neither Jew nor Greek, slave nor free, male nor female, for
> you are all one in Christ Jesus. (Galatians 3:28)

> (you) have put on the new self, which is being renewed in knowl-
> edge in the image of its Creator. Here there is no Greek or Jew, cir-
> cumcised or uncircumcised, barbarian, Scythian, slave or free, but
> Christ is all, and is in all. (Colossians 3:10–11)

Now of course these ideas are important. All Christians have 'dual citizenship'. While we live in this world we are citizens of an earthly country. Our ultimate destiny, however, lies in being citizens of heaven. The Kingdom of God is what we seek to bring to people's lives, with all it involves in terms of salvation, healing and wholeness. Jesus is Lord of that Kingdom and he deserves final honour from us. Equally, Christianity is the great leveler. True status comes from our being children of God, not whether we are of a certain nationality or gender or social status. Within the church, the body of Christ here on earth, we are not to treat each other better or worse according to earthy standards. We are indeed 'renewed in knowledge of the image of our Creator' and 'all one in Christ Jesus.'

But the reality is that we need to recognise that human beings are incredibly varied. We *do* have different national characteristics, and there are differences within nations and societies. It's when those differences of culture, language, accent, or whatever are allowed to prejudice us that we go against the Gospel of Christ. If we can celebrate all these things it's a different matter. I love accents, for example. I actually love mimicking them and people say I'm quite good at it. When I do, it's not because I'm knocking someone or making fun of them but because I enjoy their accent and get pleasure from imitating it. Unfortunately, I have to be very careful because not everybody understands this!

In Genesis 11 there is the story of the Tower of Babel, where God confuses the languages of people so that they can't aspire to be like him. Many have taken this as proof that people are not meant to speak different languages, and one could easily argue that many conflicts and misunderstandings could have been avoided if we were able to communicate better. However, this is not a watertight argument, and the story in Genesis is really all about the pride of man and the greatness of God rather than an argument against languages. The fact is, we have to live with differences and we can choose to decry them or to celebrate them.

These differences are not just about language, of course. Culture is about a whole host of things that make a group of people distinct. It can be clothes, the food you eat or the way you eat, attitudes towards family, marriage and gender, and on another level temperament and sense of humour. Often these things don't cause us any problems, especially if we've been used to living in a multicultural environment. We might make light of the fact that we British have a more 'stiff upper lip' than, say, people from Mediterranean countries. We might joke that we don't understand the French or the Italians.

At other times they are much more important than we realise. Thankfully, most mission societies understand this these days. The Gospel is no longer packaged in the culture of the country sending the missionaries, imposing ways of worship and lifestyles that owe more to that culture than they do to the Gospel. Anyone wishing to engage with another people needs to understand about them. You can never generalise of course; just because people come from a country in Africa doesn't mean they have the same culture as those from another country, and of course there will be differences based on all sorts of other things. Northern Europeans may generally be emotionally less demonstrative than southern Europeans, perhaps, but it would be presumptuous if I assumed I knew all about Scandinavians for example.

Much is being said today as well of how the Gospel is to relate to all the various subcultures within our own society. So-called 'fresh expressions' of church are springing up in order to engage with people for whom traditional church is completely foreign. I have had the privilege of being part of a church that planted a new congregation in a youth centre based around a skate park. It has reached young unchurched people for Christ and drawn them into his Kingdom in a way that traditional church struggles to do. It was a huge undertaking for us as an ordinary church, but we believed we were just being obedient to the Lord's command to go into *all* the world with the good news.[1]

Wounded history

So how important is it to think about where we're from? As with all these factors, we shouldn't give it more importance than it's worth, but at the same time it can have an effect on attitudes and emotional behaviour. If you're proud to come from a certain country, or a certain county, village or city, then that's great. As long as you don't think you're better than someone else just because of that. Quite often it's the other way around, and people can be a bit self-conscious about where they come from. Maybe they come from somewhere perceived as not very nice by other people. Birmingham isn't a bad place to live. It has nice suburbs, a city centre being developed much more for tourism, and more trees than most cities I've been to. However, I've met an awful lot of people who have never been there and still have an image of it being a dour and grubby manufacturing town.

Sometimes people have a chip on their shoulder without realising it. I'm proud to be half Welsh, but it's interesting that my mother never spoke Welsh to me when I was little. In those days it was considered less socially acceptable, and there's no doubt that many people who left Wales did so with a view to 'bettering' themselves. I have met Welsh people of a certain generation who almost seem to want to hide their Welshness. Of course, it's equally true that expatriates can become the most patriotic people of all. At the same time, there are attitudes amongst many Welsh people towards the English that have their origins in economic and social dominance by the English, including the attempt to destroy the use of the Welsh language, way back in history. There is a deep resentment that some can articulate, and others not. I always remember my uncle Moelwyn declaring that he didn't mind the Welsh rugby team being beaten as long as it wasn't by the English!

Russ Parker deals with this sort of thing in his book *Healing Wounded History* [2]. He also mentions a couple of times this attitude amongst many Welsh people. We might joke about the rugby, but actually some of these feelings go very deep. Sometimes they're not always obvious, but you don't have to scratch too far beneath the surface to find them. Of course, I'm only talking about something I have some experience of; there are many examples of deep hurt, not only amongst nation groups but also amongst communities, families, and indeed churches.

I want to talk about families in particular later on, but the whole purpose of discussing these things now is simply to remind us that we haven't just come from anywhere. History has an influence on us. Russ Parker very helpfully talks about the power of 'group memory' and the things that shape the stories of groups of people. He speaks of the value of research, of finding out what makes a place tick, in order to help in mission in that place. It has become more common in recent times for Christians in particular to apologise for the sins of the past and to repent on behalf of those perceived to have sinned against other groups. The slave trade, years of oppression in Ireland, the Highland clearances in Scotland, and the subjugation of the American Indians are just a few that come to mind. Sometimes these are far in the past, but in many cases the memories are still real even if pushed into the background.

A feudal place

It's always worth trying to understand how people's mental attitudes have been shaped by the past. Sometimes it's the history of the actual place, perhaps the effects of past strife. As Russ Parker reminds us, the very ground itself isn't neutral and can affect the spirituality of a place. However, my particular interest is more how we can be aware of the effects on ourselves as individuals of the place we live in or where we come from. It may be spiritual or it may be emotional, but then the two can be intertwined anyway.

I think, for example, of the two places where I have had the 'cure of souls', to put it in the language of the Church of

England. I was the Rector for eight years of two parishes in the south of Somerset. The larger village of Templecombe, where we lived as a family, was a mixture of original Somerset people and those who had moved there. Some of these came to work in the area, some to commute as far as London, others to live there at weekends, and quite a few to retire. The congregation included many of these 'incomers'. Those in the congregation who were Somerset people by upbringing tended to have had longstanding links with the church. Others in the village, however, were quite hard to reach with the Gospel. It was never actually expressed openly, but Jane and I detected an ambiguous attitude from these people towards the church. It wasn't just because we were from outside.

Never having lived in the countryside before, my knowledge of how rural parishes grew up was fairly limited. Templecombe was unusual in that it grew considerably in the 1860s as a railway village, when the Somerset and Dorset line was built to cross the main Southern Railway line from London to Exeter at that location. There was a mixture of those who worked on the land and those who were connected with the railway. My other parish, Horsington, was generally more well-to-do. The original Rector there was wealthy, but there were a couple of other families that were wealthier.

In Templecombe, the family that produced a long line of Rectors right up to the 1920s was the wealthiest in the parish. I wouldn't doubt the effectiveness or the loyalty of their ministry for a moment, but I have no doubt that the wealth factor created an invisible barrier. We lived in a very modest 1960s Rectory, but the old Rectory was enormous and set in several acres of land. Of course, there would have been servants and the old system of the locals providing the tithe from the land would have been in operation even to a surprisingly late date.

The family 'dynasty' ended after the two older sons were killed in the First World War and the youngest son refused to become ordained. Instead, he went into teaching, much to the displeasure of his father. I actually met this son not long after I went there. He still kept an interest in the place after all those years. When he died, the funeral was held in the church and an ordained family friend delivered the tribute, which included fascinating details of what life was like in an Edwardian Rectory.

The whole nature of this setup became clear to me one day when I was talking to an old member of the choir. He was reminiscing about the times when the choir boys were invited once a year to an 'open house' at the Rectory, and the Rector's wife would treat them to lemon cordial in the garden. These were very special occasions indeed, and they were the only times when he went anywhere near the place. As far as I could ascertain, it was the same for most of the locals. It was hardly surprising that generations of villagers should grow up with a kind of feudal attitude, with the Rector occupying a position almost akin to the lord of the manor.

Far be it from me to criticise the way things were done in the past, nor the people involved. I know there was a faithful Christian witness for centuries in that place. But I'm convinced it left a legacy whereby people still saw the Rector and his wife as belonging to a different class. Despite giving everyone permission to call me by my first name, many found that extremely difficult. I know that this is true in many places still today, including towns and cities. People simply do not know how to talk to the Vicar or Rector and it's taking a long time to change the image. In an old parish like Templecombe it seemed particularly marked.

There were other issues in the place, including the history of the Knights Templar who had been there in the Middle Ages. How much spiritual legacy remained from that was unclear, although it was often in our thoughts when praying about mission and so on. However, I felt that this subconscious barrier between church and village was an issue to be very much aware of and to be brought constantly to the Lord.

From Wessex to Essex

At the time of writing we have lived for a number of years in a parish in the south of Essex. This has been a complete change from rural Somerset. The parish is in Benfleet, a town of some forty thousand people. The county itself has a rich history, but the area along the Thames Gateway where Benfleet is situated has grown up since the 1950s and '60s as people have moved out from East London. As a result, the area is predominantly white first, second and third generation Eastenders. The people are very open and friendly. Many work in manual occupations, with tradesmen parking their vans (often white, I have to say) outside their houses at night.

Like anywhere, there are many issues below the surface. Our borough has below national average figures for those in tertiary education. I often detect people struggling with a bit of an inferiority complex, which I'm convinced goes back to the East End. For generations the people there were hard-working, 'salt of the earth' folk, who never really had the prospect of rising above their station. The rest of London was in many ways seen as superior. This has led not only to the sense of inferiority but also to a suspicion of authority. Occasionally this can surface as a kind of 'inverted snobbery'.

There is also the whole aspect of people discovering a new freedom. Over the last forty or fifty years people have at last been able to move away from the city. They've had relatively more disposable income, and although now the reality is that people are in debt far more than they were, people still like spending money. I think it's significant that we have Lakeside, the largest shopping centre and retail park in Europe, just down the road, while our local Tesco store is, at the time of writing anyway, the biggest in Britain.

So the real 'history' issues are more to do with where people have come from originally, rather than the land itself. I'm convinced that they need to be taken into account when sharing the Gospel in this part of the world and in dealing with people's personal issues. Of course they're not the whole story and I'm generalising and simplifying a lot. Nevertheless, communal 'story' – of history, hang-ups, humour and a host of other things – must be a big part of what makes us us.

I've tried to think about all this in relation to myself. It hasn't provided all the answers, of course, but it's yet something else to invite the Holy Spirit to share, and when necessary to bring healing. For me, I know there's been something of a rebelliousness within me towards authority. Some psychologists would put this down to my family situation, but just as easily it could be part of my identity inherited from the Welsh community. On the other hand, I'm half English, so I don't truly fit in either side of the divide. Having been brought up in a so-called 'provincial' city has probably given me a bit of a chip on my shoulder and I know I've had to allow the Spirit to release me from wrong attitudes towards Londoners and the southeast of England in general. It's probably just as well considering where the Lord called us to minister!

Sociological background

Systems

In many ways this overlaps with the last main section, since some of the things I've been talking about are really about the sociological make-up of groups of people. I realise that sociology is a big science, and to talk about class on its own is not adequate. However, with all the changes and issues in society that have happened in my lifetime, I'm convinced this is still a very real issue. It's not a terribly politically correct thing to talk about class these days but I believe that it, or at least how we *perceive* it (even if incorrectly), is still an issue to consider in what makes me me.

Of course this is going to differ from culture to culture. In India for example, the caste system was officially disbanded in 1948. However, it still features in many people's thinking throughout Hindu society. This previously unalterable system owed its existence to the belief in karma, whereby people were reincarnated at a level of existence that rewarded or punished them according to how they performed in their previous life. The highest caste were the Brahmins, the lowest the Sudras, with outcasts or untouchables basically off the scale. You were what you were born, and in this life, at least, you couldn't change things.

It wasn't that long ago in our own society in Britain that people had a similar way of thinking, although it was possible to climb socially of course, and many did throughout the Industrial Revolution for example. Many people believed that you were born to a particular class, and that was it. In his political treatise of 1843, *Past and Present*, the Scotsman Thomas Carlyle wrote, 'Blessed is he who has found his work; let him ask no other blessedness.' Part of his analysis of how society should be is that each person is born to his or her particular state, and should find satisfaction in taking their place in the natural order of society. Naturally charismatic leaders should be allowed to rise up as they had in previous heroic ages. Of course, this is the exact opposite of democracy.

We perhaps should not be surprised to learn that Adolf Hitler admired Carlyle's work. The basis of National Socialism was that there was a natural order of things in humanity, from the ruling classes of the master race down to the Untermenschen, or sub-humans, such as the Jews or Romanies. Within that system, each was to be proud to take his or her place in building the Reich, and ultimately of course the subclasses were not only expendable but needed to be eliminated in order to ensure a pure society.

I'm not suggesting that the class system in Britain ever could have led to that, but nevertheless the underlying psyche for generations allowed for people to remain either in various degrees of power or of subjugation. The hymn 'All things bright and beautiful' is still popular today, even at weddings. I wonder how many of us would be comfortable nowadays to sing the second verse that appeared originally in *Hymns for Little Children* in 1848:

> The rich man in his castle,
> The poor man at his gate,
> God made them, high or lowly,
> And ordered their estate.

The legacy

Some sort of class system exists in most societies, even after attempts to eliminate it. Even communism didn't succeed in overcoming human nature when it came to privileges for the few. As the pigs in Orwell's *Animal Farm* declare, 'All animals are equal, but some animals are more equal than others.' Even in the more affluent western nations, where opportunities exist to increase living standards for more people than ever, we are still left with the idea that some people are better than others.

Whether this is a legacy of the past or whether it really is just down to natural human inclinations doesn't matter for my purposes as much as the effect it has on each of us. I'm sure that many of us will be shaped in our attitudes and emotions by a class psyche to a degree, even if it's subconscious. The problem is, it's a very elusive phenomenon to describe, especially in a country like Britain, which we might describe as 'modern' or 'developed' and yet has a long history.

Before the Second World War people were possibly more comfortable with labels. Even for somebody like me, born in the 1950s, it was not unusual to hear people described as 'working-class', 'middle-class', 'upper middle-class', or 'upper-class'. The assumption was that it had something to do with money, or a least the type of job you did. It might have had something to do with the kind of school you went to, or the way you spoke. If you spoke with a Received Pronunciation accent ('posh' to most people) it was assumed that you probably had more money than others, were better educated, and certainly lived in a bigger house. A doctor would normally be posh, a teacher slightly less so, and a labourer or factory worker definitely not.

I mentioned earlier that I'm fascinated by accents, and it's amazing how many different ones there are in a relatively small country like Britain, along with all kinds of variations. A survey in the UK in 2005 by The Aziz Corporation found that regional accents can be 'bad for business'. It revealed deep prejudices in the business world towards the way people speak. Apparently, among English accents associated with business failure are Liverpudlian, Birmingham or West Midlands, Cockney, Geordie and the West Country. On the other hand, seventy-seven per cent of business people thought a Home Counties (that is, around London) accent was a sign of success in business. That doesn't come as a surprise to me. I've always been aware that many people have associated a Birmingham, or Brummie, accent with being perhaps not as intelligent as others. It's been called a 'lazy' accent, yet to my ear very few actors and actresses seem clever enough to put one on convincingly!

It's obvious that prejudices like this go far deeper than simply assessing people on whether they have money or not. As I said, thankfully many more people from all sorts of backgrounds have found opportunities to better themselves financially in recent years. The whole thing is actually very complex and I'm not sure that any experts have really managed to assess or describe society adequately in these terms. Many people would prefer to say that we are classless, and yet most of us know instinctively that this isn't true. Whenever we meet someone, we assess them in all sorts of ways, of which their accent is just one. There are attitudes towards bringing up children we might find ourselves prejudiced about; indeed we might even assess somebody by what names they gave their children! There are attitudes to how people spend money rather than how much they have that may colour how we think about them. How people dress says something to us, or how they decorate their home, the sort of food they eat, their leisure pursuits. The list goes on.

Eyes open

Why should this be so important? Well, for a start we all know that prejudice is not a good thing. A bias or an opinion about something or someone that is preconceived, wherever that preconception comes from, means that we're not allowing ourselves to relate to that thing or person in a way that is free. In fact the opposite is true, that we are bound up by thoughts and emotions and in turn bind up others. This is true for everyone, and we know the world would be a better place without such prejudice.

It's important for Christians to share God's love adequately, not just to believe that the Gospel is for everyone but also to be able to proclaim and demonstrate it across all man-made boundaries. The Bible doesn't pull any punches in speaking about this:

> If you really keep the royal law found in Scripture, 'Love your neighbour as yourself,' you are doing right. But if you show favouritism, you sin and are convicted by the law as law-breakers. (James 2:8–9)

Once again, it's all about inviting the Holy Spirit to put you in touch with what you're feeling and being honest with him and with yourself. Then you can ask him to set you free to love others as you're meant to.

Any of us that say we're not prejudiced in some way are not being honest. I look at my own background and realise it's very different to others. I was brought up in a nice suburb by parents who were in reasonable professions, if not the most highly paid. I was brought up to save money. I had a little metal box owned by the Birmingham Municipal Bank into which I put money whenever I could. Despite what I perceived as financial insecurities after my father left, it was a huge revelation to me when I started working for the DHSS to come across people who never saved a penny of their weekly giro. They lived from week to week in a way that was completely foreign to my 'middle middle-class' background. I struggled not to think the worst of them. In the light of my working class ancestry that's quite ironic. It's just one example of things I still need to bring to the Lord for continual sorting out.

Two-way prejudices

These perceived differences not only prevent us from treating others as we should, but they can colour the way we perceive ourselves. Of course it depends which circles you mix in, and no doubt there are plenty of people who see themselves as better than others because of their upbringing. For many people, however, it's a case either of being convinced that they're not good enough, or of feeling they have to prove something in life. This might manifest itself as what we often call 'a chip on the shoulder', which most people tend to spot a mile off because people come across as very prickly characters. It might well add to a person's 'inferiority complex'.

I'm actually very grateful for having been brought into contact with quite a wide range of 'class', for want of a much better word. I think that having been involved in Christian circles from a fairly young age has helped here. My involvement with those youth meetings in the centre of Birmingham was the first time I ever mixed with people who had been to public school. I remember going with Nick Cuthbert to sing at a public school in Worcestershire one evening. Nick told me that we would be having supper with the staff and pupils. Now, from my background 'supper' meant something you had before going to bed; a light meal, perhaps a biscuit or toast. I remember thinking, 'Surely we're not going to be there that late.' You see, 'supper' in public school meant a cooked evening meal. I always thought that was dinner. In fact, when I was young I used to eat lunch at dinnertime and dinner at teatime. Now how confusing is all that!

We can laugh at these little differences in British culture, but actually there can be quite serious ramifications. When I was young all I ever really knew of people who spoke with 'posh' accents was what I'd seen in films or on television. Mostly, they were the sort of people I would regard as pretty unapproachable. Despite having gone to a grammar school, only one or two teachers spoke like that, and they probably fitted the bill in my eyes. However, the more Christians I met who spoke that way, the more I realised how wrong I was. Many, many people who weren't quite like me were some of the loveliest people you could meet, especially the Christians. Snobbery has nothing to do with the way you speak; it's an attitude. God uses people from all kinds of background.

Having said that, I feel quite strongly about the general failure of the Church of England to reach those who are not of a 'middle-class' background. There are all sorts of reasons for this, including how people are selected for training for ordination and leadership, and the kind of teaching and worship on offer. This affects things at both local church level and larger events. Even when it comes to things like the enormously successful *Alpha* course we have to be careful about presentation. Certain things need to be adapted for use in places that are not like Knightsbridge. In the light of what I said above, for example, is it an *Alpha* supper or an *Alpha* dinner at teatime?

When Jane and I became involved with St. John's Harborne we mixed with quite a range of people, and later at theological college in Bristol. Later on again, we were to experience an amazing range of people in a relatively small benefice in Somerset. Here we were to meet people who worked in farming or who had worked on the railways as well as military 'types' and even aristocracy. I'll never forget making the acquaintance of Lady Lettice McCreery, the widow of General Sir Richard McCreery, who had eventually commanded the British Eighth Army in Italy in the Second World War. She was a Lady in her own right by birth. To me, she was extremely posh and some people found her quite formidable. However, I knew her simply as a lovely Christian who joined with us in a monthly prayer meeting for the sick. At her rather grand funeral in Sherborne Abbey I was able to speak about that in addition to the more historical tribute given about her.

Thanks to experiences like that, I like to think that any chip on my shoulder has been fairly well removed. Nevertheless, I'm so aware of the problems this whole scenario gives to people. Once again, all I'm really trying to say is that we need to be aware of the influences upon us that can lead to all sorts of feelings within us and reactions to other people. I believe the Gospel of Jesus Christ and the power of his Holy Spirit are all about revealing to us the true worth of *all* people, regardless of their backgrounds, and that we can be secure in the knowledge that we are simply brothers and sisters together, with no need for inferiority or superiority complexes. It brings us back to Paul's words in Colossians 3:11, which are worth repeating: 'Here there is no Greek or Jew, circumcised or uncircumcised, barbarian, Scythian, slave or free, but Christ is all, and is in all.'

Social Trauma

Tied in with the whole idea of where you're from, the community you belong to or have come from, is the fact that many groups of people have gone through what I call 'social trauma'. At the risk of repeating what have already said, it's fairly important to remember that group memory can be carried on through the generations, along with prejudices, anger or resentment. I'm thinking more here again, however, of how events in history might have affected each of us on an individual level. What have we inherited through circumstances?

The best way to illustrate what I mean is to think about my own parents. As a baby boomer, I have grown up in a peaceful Europe. There have been many wars elsewhere in the world, but nothing to affect me personally. When I conduct funerals of anyone born before the Second World War however, I often reflect on how they might have coped and what a difference the upheaval of that time must have made on their lives. I've always been interested in the Second World War. When I was little it was all about playing soldiers and making models of aeroplanes and tanks. There is still something of the little boy in me I admit, but mostly my interest now is to try and imagine what it was really like either to fight or to keep going in ordinary everyday life.

I think it's vitally important for us all to know about the history of the period not long before we were born. It's too easy for a generation to repeat the mistakes of the past. We need to *know* about the Holocaust and other events, in a sense to let them live in us so that they become part of our psyche. No one generation exists in a vacuum. I often think about what it must have been like for my parents. My mother was only sixteen when war broke out. I remember her telling us how she went out with a Polish boy before she moved from Wales. He was in bomber command and never returned from a raid. She met my father during the war. He was only a year older than her and was to spend much of the time away fighting in the Army. Even when they married just after the war he was immediately posted to India for three months.

What was it like to be in your late teens and early twenties during such a frightening and uncertain time? How much did my mother fear about my dad not returning? He himself spoke very little about the war when we were children. Once when I was older I remember him describing how in battle you'd see friends dying every day and your constant thought was whether you'd be the next to 'cop it'. How does that affect someone long-term, and how do they adjust to life when they return home?

I suppose I'll never know the answers about all this as far as my father was concerned. Any difficulties he may have had in relating to his wife, or even to people in general, may have stemmed from much earlier. After all, many did return from fighting and have long and happy marriages. Nevertheless, I often wondered about the effect of such collective social trauma and how that in a way has had a knock-on effect upon me.

The twentieth century was one of massive upheaval, and I think some historians are justified in saying that the Second World War was in many ways a continuation of the Great War, since Germany remained so dissatisfied after 1918. When my father died in 2005, my brother and I attended his funeral. There were not many people there, which was of course sad anyway, and it was quite a strange experience for us as our relationship with him had been so difficult. However, it was very therapeutic to spend time afterwards with our half brother and half sister going through photographs and swapping experiences. My mother had destroyed most of the photographs of my father when he left, and certainly I didn't possess any. It was nice to have a couple, including one of my father in Italy in his corporal's uniform.

My paternal grandfather's suicide was never really spoken about in our family, although there was some mention of bankruptcy being involved. I never gave it much thought. Indeed, I didn't even know my grandfather's name or what he looked like until we were going through my father's few possessions after his own death. We came across photographs of a man none of us recognised. In one he was dressed in a corporal's uniform, but this time it was of the First World War. We assumed that this was our grandfather. We learned from my father's birth certificate that his name was Hubert. As I said earlier I've since learned some more about his family line.

Various questions have gone through my mind as I've looked at this photograph on occasions. I know little about him, except some research has uncovered the fact that he enlisted twice for the Army in the Great War and was discharged twice on medical grounds. His second spell of service was for eight months but apparently he didn't fight on the front. I wonder how someone so desperate to join up was affected by not being able to be more involved. Survivors of war sometimes speak of their guilt at surviving when so many of their friends didn't. Fighting or not, it was a difficult time for all. Of course I'll never know how the chain of events might have worked. My point is that, as a result of what happened with his life and untimely death, my father was affected by losing *his* father when he was very young. This in turn could have affected me.

That's part of my story and really it's guesswork; that's all it really can be. Nevertheless, I've brought it before the Lord in prayer and asked for the wounds of the past to be healed and for me to be set free on an individual level from those collective traumas that affected so many. Of course, many others suffered in different ways and much worse. I'm sure there's still a legacy left among large parts of the population from being blitzed in the Second World War, for example. Such events are bound to leave a deep scar on more than the generation directly involved. They could have led to irrational fears in some people, or to a hardening of emotions in others (the 'grit your teeth and get on with life' mindset).

In the end, it doesn't help in any way to dwell on these things or feel hard done by because of them. Each of us has our own story of what has affected us. It may not be war of course; poverty, migration, persecution, the list goes on. We simply need to remember that the things that have moulded us to become the people we are may have their roots in a time well before we were born.

Notes

1. Details of this can be found online at www.legacyweb.org.
2. Russ Parker, *Healing Wounded History*, (Dartman Longman and Todd, 2001).

CHAPTER EIGHT

FAMILY INFLUENCES
What makes me me? 3

When I consider your heavens, the work of your fingers, the moon
and the stars, which you have set in place, what is man that you are
mindful of him, the son of man that you care for him? (Psalm 8:3–4)

The need to be brave

So far in the consideration of what makes me me we've thought
about some things that are perhaps best described as 'background', factors that might affect us from a time before we were
even born – our genetic make-up, our personality type, our
male/female differences. We've also thought about the more
collective things – the place we're from, the kind of social background we have, the traumas of whole peoples that may have
had an effect on us.

I'd like now to turn to factors that some people might regard
as 'closer to home' in a sense; experiences that have happened
to us in life, perhaps things that we might be a bit more aware
of, even if we've pushed them under the surface. Once again, I
can only emphasise that this is not a comprehensive description of human beings and their condition. I'm simply trying to
remind us how complicated we are and how much we need to
place ourselves in God's hands.

Sometimes it's too painful to face up to things or to challenge
them. For example, there may be dysfunctions in our family

127

situation that we simply don't see because we've been part of that family ever since we can remember and we know nothing else. Or if we do see a difficulty, to face up to it might cut across feelings of loyalty and love we have for other family members. If there have been traumas in our life, such as I'm having to describe about my own life in this book, it may simply be too upsetting to revisit the memories concerned.

Sometimes, we may feel that it's too painful to face up to ourselves; it's like having a splinter that gives us pain, but to remove it requires just that little bit too much bravery! However, the fact is that if we're to grow as human beings and as children of God, we have to be brave at times. It's all a question of choice; are we happy to stay where we are or do we really want to move on?

Families

Dealing with now

Many would say that our families are actually part of what is completely beyond our control. In terms of the history of our family this might be true, and so much family behaviour has an historical background to it. Whether it be patterns of behaviour inherited through the sins of our forebears, traumatic events or simply ongoing relational difficulties, it's helpful to remember that they have come together to make us who we are.

> . . . we do need to recognise that every family has its story and that as its living representatives we must know it, and be a channel for bringing healing and transformation to the repeating patterns which still damage and hurt us.
>
> Whatever the status of our family story, it is beyond question that it has a repeating pattern for good or ill.[1]

Although I've spoken about being aware of the past, and knowing as much as we can so it can be brought to the Lord for healing, the fact is that most of us will probably never find out lots of facts. In our culture this will probably become truer as time goes by and family life in our society continues to change drastically. It may become far more difficult for people to trace back through their father's history, for example. I never had a stepfather, but many children today are living with a second or even third stepfather, such is the social climate we live in. It may be easier to look at a mother's history, but even so many people simply don't have the time to do so.

What's important is to look at the relationships in the family that we *do* know about, because we've lived with them all our lives. Of course this is hard, but not impossible. It is always easier to assess others. I noticed things about my wife's family, even before we were married, that she couldn't see herself. She in turn could see things about my mother, for example, that I couldn't. For us, it's about trying to learn not to get frustrated or angry about what we might see, but about talking through issues, trying to step back and be objective in order to understand. Then, where necessary, we might pray together about things.

Families can bring great blessings or great curses. They are the places where we cut our teeth. We don't choose our parents or our siblings, yet we have a choice whether to get on with them or not. Healthy families are not necessarily where everything is always quiet and peaceful; rather they will be places of lively, even dramatic, interaction at times. How much we learn from that interaction will determine the process of maturing properly. In this context, I think it's worth remembering the words of Carl Jung: 'Everything that irritates us about others can lead to an understanding of ourselves.'

Baggage

When two people get married, they marry each other not their families. Many couples need to be reminded of this. The second major thing the Bible says about men and women, after the fact that they were created, is that a man and a woman will be united. Before that can happen, something else must take place: 'For this reason a man will leave his father and mother and be united to his wife, and they will become one flesh' (Genesis 2:24).

The man will *leave* his father and mother. It's so fundamental. One assumes it implies that a woman will leave her parents too. It doesn't take a genius to know that many marital problems stem from one partner not really making the emotional step of leaving his or her parents and the other partner becoming resentful.

I'm very aware that in speaking about families in relation to marriage I won't be making sense to everybody. Many people don't get married or live with someone, and within the church too there will be those still seeking a partner or indeed whom God has called to be single in life. However, all of us can still learn more about how our families have shaped us and how we need to discern that which is good and that which is unhelpful about them. It's simply that for the majority of people their situation is to be in partnership with someone, either in marriage or in some form of committed relationship. As it happens, it's being in a close bond with someone that grinds our rough edges together, and brings to the surface some of the family-generated reactions and emotions that can actually cause problems for that relationship if they're not dealt with openly and honestly.

Whenever two people come together in marriage, they bring with them a huge amount of baggage. When you think even of all the factors we've considered so far, it's not surprising that marriage is an enormously volatile melting pot. Sadly, many people don't face up to that fact when they get married. They believe that because they're in love that will be enough to see them through. The fact is, marriage is one long learning process and we never take the L-plates off. Couples have to work at it.

Most couples I see for marriage preparation will say that they're good at communicating, but I think the truth is most of us are very bad at it. We're not good at understanding what makes us tick, let alone the person we share our lives with every day. People often end up seeing the faults in their partner without realising their own, and indeed that their own faults can even be the *same* as their partner's. Many psychologists believe that we actually choose our partners because in some way they are like us. There may be differences in personality and how we live our lives in day-to-day detail, things that may complement each other or strengths that make up for each other's weaknesses. But generally speaking, we will have been attracted to someone because consciously or subconsciously we have seen things in them that we relate to or are somehow familiar to us.

Screens

So what is this baggage we bring? Well of course it can be an enormous number of things, including all that historical and sociological material I've talked about. Much of the time, however, it's about emotions that haven't been sorted out. Robin Skynner talks at length about the stages we go through in our development within families. I want to talk more about life stages in the next section, but here we're talking particularly about relating to family and what happens if something goes wrong.

For example, there can be problems if a mother is unable to give a baby the love he or she needs because of her own needs, perhaps through postnatal depression or some other difficulty:

> . . . There *are* some women who are not able to give the child as much love, in the sense of emotional contact, as he needs . . . The reason she can't empathise with the baby is because her own *babyhood experiences were painful*. Which means *her mother* couldn't tune in to *her* . . . And *her* mother didn't give enough to *her*, all the way back generation after generation. It's called a cycle of deprivation.[2]

Again, I want to talk about these sorts of experiences, the traumas of 'deprivation' we might go through, later on. The point here is that if these difficulties are inherited in a family they affect everyone in that family to a degree. Mainly, the reason is because they are not recognised. This is what Skynner says:

> If we miss out a stage (of development) and don't go through a substitute experience, the emotions that we haven't learned to handle will feel very awkward to us. So we're likely to start by trying to hide them from others, and end up by concealing them even from ourselves. We 'screen them off' and then we don't even realise they're there . . .
>
> . . . Every family regards some emotions as bad and screens those off. The child learns to follow suit because he risks parental rejection if he displays the taboo emotions; they feel 'bad'. So the pattern gets handed on down the family . . . And from generation to generation, too . . . Because if the children haven't learned to handle an emotion, they won't be able to help *their* children to handle it either.[3]

So, here we are hiding things as families. We're hiding our feelings because we don't know what to do with them. Take anger for example. I don't believe there's anything wrong with anger, as long as it's dealt with appropriately. A parent may get angry with a child quite justifiably, and it may lead to some sort of discipline. As long as there is some communication as to why the parent got angry, the child understands what was wrong, and there's plenty of making up with hugs and so on, then the anger need not be interpreted in any other way than as a warning against specific inappropriate behaviour. However, the parent may simply get angry because of frustration or whatever and that anger is expressed time and time again, possibly with violence or possibly with words that condemn the child as inherently naughty and generally hopeless. It's fairly obvious what long-term effect that will have on the child. He or she will not only have a very poor self-image, but they may in turn find themselves angry and yet never be able to talk about it.

It's more complicated when nobody actually gets angry. Perhaps we're in a family where rather than getting angry back, people just get 'hurt'. They take the whole thing incredibly personally. This can even happen if a child gets angry with a parent. The parent might say they're hurt, or without realising may show it. This can lead to an enormous guilt feeling in the child. After all, Mum and Dad are supposed to be stronger than me; why then can't they cope with my little tantrum? Because of the guilt, the child feels that anger is wrong, and so the emotion is put behind the screen; it's a complete taboo, a no-go area. And so the whole system is perpetuated, generation after generation.

This is an extremely simple example and usually the whole thing is much more complicated. For example, it might not be outright anger that's the problem, rather the whole idea of conflict in any form. There may be an inability actually to say what you think if you disagree, for fear subconsciously of what you'll do to the person you're disagreeing with. That person could be a sibling or even a parent. What they're really doing is playing emotional games, although they don't realise it. The consequence is that a child grows up without the ability to deal with conflict in all sorts of forms. I'm not saying for a minute that rowing and arguing all the time are good in a marriage, but I'd rather see a bit of honesty through the letting out of emotions rather than couples building up resentment and allowing small things to become big things through lack of communication.

Whose family is perfect?

So many people today are fearful of being inadequate parents. In some ways it's not a bad thing that people should think seriously about parenthood, but it's sad that people should feel so unguided. A whole industry has grown up around family psychology, with many books on the subject and a host of popular TV programmes that make much of people's fears and confusion. Whatever we think of Jerry Springer and all the other programmes that his has spawned, there's no doubt there is a fascination about the difficulties in relationships within families. Whenever people become voyeurs of others, they need to remember that very few families are anywhere near perfect.

Like everyone else, I find myself struggling to think about my own family. What were we like when I was a child? Did we fail to deal with conflict? Coming from Wales, I wonder how much my mother reflected the traditional matriarchal Welsh family set-up. Undoubtedly, she was a strong personality and able to express opinions and feelings better than my father. She always referred to 'phoning home' when she called her parents, and although I didn't think about it at the time I really wonder what my father made of that. His problem was if he couldn't express his feelings.

Conversely, did she ever really leave home in the truest sense? Underneath a strong exterior, what needs was she feeling? I'll probably never know the answers to these questions, nor how I might have been affected even if any of them are the right questions to ask. I don't know whether my parents argued very much or whether they brushed things under the carpet. I suspect the former, although I have no strong memories of it all.

I've sometimes wondered if my mother's background affected how she saw men in any way. If she were the stronger of the two in the marriage, was that because she was used to females being stronger? I do know that she hoped to see a female grandchild in her time, having had two sons herself, because she said as much. I think my nephews and my own son are great. I'm very proud of my son who was born to us first, but I remember being particularly pleased to tell my mother when my first daughter was born (she didn't live to see my second daughter).

I've found myself asking even whether she had hoped that her own second-born child would be a girl and that maybe she was slightly disappointed. She never said that to me and I may be way off the mark, but I do remember living for a long time with the thought that I wasn't as good as my older brother. My mother was never particularly good at praising me, but I put this down over the years simply to her being part of the generation to which she belonged. Much has been said in recent times by family 'experts' of the need to praise the child from a very early age. I don't think people did that so much in the 1950s and '60s, just as picking up a young baby whenever it cried wasn't the done thing. I'll come back to that later.

Meanwhile, I'm left with a lot of unanswerable questions, which it probably isn't helpful to dwell on. What's important, once again, is to bring any such suggestions before God and say, 'Lord, you know my family and my history far better than I do. Let your Spirit heal me of any past hurt, of the result of any conflicts within my family. Continue to reveal to me things that have been hidden behind a screen; help me to understand and deal with them that any pattern of dysfunction may not be passed on to the next generation.'

That may be a rather grand prayer, but I do believe the Lord can heal even where it is not possible for us to revisit the past, as it were. After all, he created families and he is in the business of restoring and renewing that which has fallen:

> A father to the fatherless, a defender of widows,
> is God in his holy dwelling.
> God sets the lonely in families,
> he leads forth the prisoners with singing.
> (Psalm 68:5–6)

Only time will tell with my children, and theirs for that matter, if I've actually learned anything about families!

Life stages

No escape

As we consider families, we can't help thinking about the various stages we all go through in life. Everyone is different, but there are bound to be marked times, periods of intense 'climbing' of the mountain after being on a plateau for a while. Sometimes people sail through these stages; however, often they can be quite traumatic, especially if things don't go quite according to plan.

Life stages can creep up on you, especially when time seems to go more quickly as you get older. When I was thinking of leaving my parishes in Somerset I went to see my Bishop, Jim Thompson. Although he was of a more liberal theological persuasion than me, he had a great pastor's heart and was very easy to get on with. We had a long chat in the garden of his home in the Bishop's Palace in Wells, during which he suggested I read a book that he wrote when he was Bishop of Stepney. He lent me his copy and to my dismay it was all about the male midlife crisis. I thought, 'He's got this wrong, I'm not at that stage yet, far from it.'

The problem was, as I read the book I kept recognising descriptions of certain things in me! I don't think Bishop Jim was trying to dissuade me from moving, but obviously one or two things I had mentioned during our chat had given him the opportunity to put me in mind of what stage I was beginning to go through. I remember going to a couple of seminars later on at successive New Wine summer conferences. The first was very helpful, thinking about how in full-time ministry mid-life can be a very productive time as we can relate to a wide age spread of people and bring experience while still having energy. The second was less helpful for me, since it seemed to be all about male impotency, and I have to say I couldn't relate to it at all. I left in rather a hurry convinced I must have gone to the wrong seminar!

The fact is, we can't escape going through life stages. It's what happens during each stage that will determine how we move on to the next one, and how we will cope with the rest of life. Even experiencing mid-life has made me think how things could have been different had I not experienced the healing and renewing power of the Holy Spirit in days gone by. For example, to be insecure in your identity as a person could easily mean floundering on the rocks when you reach a certain age. If your security has come from being youthful, from assuming you might be attractive to the opposite sex, then you might find the appearance of wrinkles and grey hairs extremely threatening to your ego. If your job or career is all that gives you credibility, then the slow realisation that you may not be as energetic or as quick-witted in the next few years might mean a 'crisis' is looming. Indeed, mid-life can bring the awareness that you're not immortal after all, and if you're not secure in your eternal destiny what a problem that can be.

I'm not pretending that mid-life can be easy to face, but I'm absolutely sure that it will be harder if previous life stages haven't gone well. I fully expect that to be true also of retirement when that stage finally comes. No matter what age we are it's never too late to seek healing, whatever self-awareness that might necessitate. It might mean 'revisiting' various stages, of going over the ground as far as we're able to remember, and inviting the Holy Spirit to heal and make whole as necessary. It's certainly no good hoping that things will eventually just turn out all right. There can be as much confusion and depression amongst older people as anyone else:

> None of us will have made the journey through the various stages perfectly . . . This is true in the process of normal growth, but where a person has failed to negotiate a developmental task at the appropriate stage the passage of time may only highlight the problem. The solution lies in going back to the task and with God's help renegotiating it. As he promised in Joel, he will repay us for the years the locusts have eaten (Joel 2:25). God is able to reparent us and make up that which has been lost or stolen from us. Our responsibility is to come into his presence and give him the opportunity to address the need within us.[4]

Formative years

Various experts over the years have attempted to divide human experience into stages. One of the better-known psychoanalysts to do this was Erik Erikson (1902–1994), who defined eight basic stages. Three of these come later on: young adulthood, middle age and older adult.

That leaves five basic stages that we could perhaps describe as belonging to our 'formative years'. It's not my intention to go into all of these here, as they would take up another book; the important thing is that we are aware that there will have been particular times in our lives when we were especially reliant on our parents or a reasonably stable family atmosphere. There may have been particular times when we have struggled to move on. Below are Erikson's stages. The age ranges are approximate:

Infant (0–12 months)
Trust v. Mistrust
The child needs maximum comfort with minimal uncertainty to trust himself/herself, others, and the environment

Toddler (15 months-3 years)
Autonomy v. Shame and Doubt
The child seeks to master his/her physical environment while maintaining self-esteem

Preschooler (3–6 years)
Initiative v. Guilt
The child begins to initiate and not merely imitate activities; he/she develops conscience and sexual identity

School-Age Child (6–12 years)
Industry v. Inferiority
The child tries to develop a sense of self-worth by refining his/her skills

Adolescent
Identity v. Role Confusion
The 'child' tries to integrate many roles (child, sibling, student, athlete, worker) into a self-image under a role model and peer pressure

Many would add a couple of other stages to these; pre-birth and birth itself. When you glance down the list of these, it makes you realise how vulnerable human beings are. All sorts of things can happen at these stages. For example, research has taken place in recent years to look at how a foetus can be affected by external influences. If the mother is stressed by something, this may be passed on to the child. We're finding out more and more how responsive the unborn child can be. The womb is meant to be a very safe and secure environment, but it surely can't be immune from external noise or even minute chemical changes in the mother's body caused, say, by stress. The other side of the coin is that it's possible that playing soothing music or speaking softly and lovingly can have a beneficial effect on the child.

How on earth do you or I know what it was like before we were born? Some research might bear fruit. For example, if we know our mother went through some difficult experience during pregnancy we might want to bring this in prayer to the Lord and ask for healing *in case* it had an effect on us. There's not a lot of point in dwelling on it, however, especially if we don't have a clue about events. The same might apply to the actual birth experience. We may know about some difficult experience at or around our birth, or more likely we'll have no idea. When we do know something, however, it's worth covering the event in prayer.

For example, my son's birth was not particularly easy, and also very soon afterwards he had to go under an ultraviolet lamp because of slight jaundice, separated for long periods from his mother. Needless to say, we prayed a lot over him after this, but we have not dwelt on it. On occasions, someone might need to 'relive' their birth event. There has been a very strong stream of psychotherapy advocating this, using a variety of techniques. Probably the best-known in Christian circles has been Frank Lake's 'clinical theology'.

Personally I think counselling that involves creating this situation has to be handled very carefully, and it shouldn't be assumed that everyone needs to go through it, but I know there are those who disagree with me. Having said that, there have been many instances recorded in recent times where people have had a spontaneous and deep experience of the Holy Spirit that has somehow taken them into that 're-birthing' experience, even assuming a foetal position on the floor in many cases.

Using the list

I think the most helpful thing to do is to look at the list of the various life stages in an attitude of prayer, thinking through and highlighting what may have been particularly important for you. We don't have to look for problems where no problems exist, but we might be aware of difficulties at a certain stage. For me, it's fairly obvious to think about the so-called 'school-age child', since the trauma of my parents splitting up happened during those years.

If Erikson was right, this was a particularly important time in terms of developing my self-worth. Quite apart from all of the self blame that might have been going on subconsciously (which I mentioned previously), it was obviously at a time when I was learning and refining skills to do with growing up as a young male. I would have needed a father around to help me in this, and of course from early in this stage he was no longer there. Needless to say, the next stage of adolescence lacked a role model to help with self-image. I think having an uncle-in-law to whom I related well helped to an extent, but he couldn't be around as much as a father.

Others might relate more to some of the earlier stages in the list. Certainly, many psychoanalysts believe that people are affected most in these initial times. Not receiving as much comfort as needed during the first twelve months of life can have a huge effect on a child. I have wondered if it's true that I was allowed to cry in my cot for long hours at a time without being picked up and comforted, as I believe was more the practice in the 1950s. It's believed that at that stage, an infant perceives he or she is the centre of the universe. Why isn't anyone stroking them, giving them the fullest attention, and making them *feel* the most important person in the world? Of course, there's no ability to verbalise these feelings on the part of the baby; they simply have an unfulfilled need, which may be taken right into adulthood. They won't be able to negotiate so easily stages of 'separation' when they realise they're not actually the centre of everything, while for others those stages are OK because they had enough attention when they were small.

It's not always as simple as a child just not being picked up. There may be more complicated things going on. For example, because of her own emotional difficulties a mother may have a need for the support and love of a child, rather than giving him or her emotional support. She may become possessive and the child finds they can't use a normal substitute (such as a teddy bear) as a support in growing naturally away from the mother. Robin Skynner describes how this can lead to a life taking a completely different direction:

> . . . There are two tracks that we can take through life. One is the 'open, relaxed' track. The other's the 'closed, uptight' one. And which track we find ourselves on is largely determined by how we and our mothers manage this separating phase between about six months and three years old . . .[5]

This whole business of 'separation' is so important. It's not just about learning to be independent of a mother, but actually separating out emotions and learning to deal with them. When a baby is young it's unable to deal with most emotions:

> . . . At this stage in the baby's development, the baby is not able to connect and balance up his emotions, so some feelings are very frightening. The baby projects these, which makes him feel better. But the world around him becomes more frightening instead.[6]

In other words, the world is very scary for a young child. Fairy stories with cruel witches and goblins reflect that, although in fact they can be a way of learning to handle unmanageable feelings. With the right care and nurture needed at this stage, the child learns to handle things. It's when that help isn't received properly that a child can get stuck at that stage, and the world then remains a very insecure place.

Obstacle race

It all feels like a bit of an obstacle race, doesn't it? Just when you've got through one stage, another looms and catches you unprepared. I've only managed to summarise things pretty inadequately again, and I would urge anyone sufficiently interested to read further on the subject. However, all of us should be aware to an extent of what has gone on in our lives at particular times. If we can look back and highlight stages where we think we might have got a bit stuck, then maybe we need to seek help. It needn't be full-blown psychotherapy, just asking someone to come alongside you and pray with you as you invite the Lord to help you revisit those times. You might need to use imagination; you certainly need the Holy Spirit. As long as you don't dwell unnecessarily on events, especially given the power of the human mind to imagine what might not really have happened.

I've spoken about certain stages that I've obviously had to revisit fairly deeply. I don't claim that I'm now perfect and able to face whatever else might come. Indeed, no one is perfect and it doesn't matter how many books you read, or how many new theories people might come up with, we all bear a certain amount of injury from trying to negotiate life. I'm not even convinced that the experts all understand the complications of life's stages, and as a race we continue to learn about ourselves. I'll finish this chapter with an interesting summary I came across of the five stages of learning that we go through in life.

The five stages of learning

1. You don't know
   And you don't realize you don't know

2. You don't know
   But you think you do know
3. You still don't know
   And you realize that you don't know
4. You know
   But you don't realize that you know
5. You know
   And you know that you know

Would that we could all reach number five at some point!

Notes

1. Russ Parker, *Healing Wounded History*, (Dartman Longman and Todd, 2001, p. 124).
2. Robin Skynner and John Cleese, *Families and How to Survive Them*, (Methuen, 1983, p. 113).
3. *Ibid*. p. 30.
4. Mary Pytches, *Yesterday's Child*, (Hodder and Stoughton, 1990, p. 142).
5. Skynner and Cleese, *op. cit.* p. 150.
6. *Ibid*. p. 99.

CHAPTER NINE

RESPONSE TO EVENTS
What makes me me? 4

We may go to the moon, but that's not very far. The greatest distance we have to cover still lies within us. Charles de Gaulle (1890–1970)

But for you who revere my name, the sun of righteousness will rise with healing in its wings. And you will go out and leap like calves released from the stall. (Malachi 4:2)

A bit of this, a bit of that

I read an amazing story about an eighty year-old grand-mother in India who allegedly eats *sand* to stay fit and healthy. Apparently, she eats lots of it, before breakfast, lunch and after-noon tea. She is reported to have told a news agency, 'When young, I tried it for fun once. Since then, I am used to it. My brothers and relatives pestered me to quit it but it was all in vain. I eat on an average around one or one-and-a-half kilos of sand per day.' Her granddaughter said: 'The doctor said if she has no health problems, let her eat. We think it suits her health.'

We live in a culture obsessed with health. People will try anything if they think it will help them to live longer. I must admit, eating sand is a new one on me, but there are neverthe-less lots of strange remedies out there. The same is true when it comes to people desiring to be whole, emotionally and spir-itually. Bookshops are full of all sorts of therapies, self-help philosophies, spiritual practices and religions. It's interesting how emotional health and spirituality overlap much more in people's thinking nowadays.

Actually, Christians have always believed in the integration of the physical, the emotional and the spiritual. The difference is that Christianity makes demands of discipleship, and challenges people's lifestyles. Because of that, many have chosen to reject it. On the other hand, the spiritualities we often put under the label New Age tend to make fewer demands, and they begin not with God but with the individual. Ours is a pick and mix generation where people choose the best bits of different faith systems and cobble together whatever suits them.

The odd thing is that I think it's not a bad thing to choose the best bits when it comes to healing therapy. I'd prefer not to take one line and always stick to that. Nevertheless, there are bound to be certain ones we come across that will either prove helpful or not. Ultimately, whatever human knowledge and ideas we choose to take on board, they should all be measured against what Scripture says about human beings and how we should live our lives in relation to God.

Before I go back to my story and specifically how the Lord dealt with me, I'd like to consider three more factors that go to make us the people we are. As before, they often overlap.

Personal Traumas

A fallen world

I suppose in a way this is a fairly obvious subject. The fact is, very few of us go through life unscathed. There will always be things we remember that were traumatic, unless they were so harrowing that our brains have somehow blanked them out. Sometimes that's the natural way our bodies deal with trauma, a survival mechanism. It might happen for example when people can't remember details of a serious accident they were involved in.

People have to learn to deal with all sorts in this world of accident and human fallenness, and of course reactions can vary enormously. As I'm writing this there have been a number of awful events in schools in the United States. In one a man killed five young girls and seriously injured several more in a school in an Amish community. Of course, people are asking why it should have happened. Even if they get something like an answer, it won't bring those children back. That community talked about forgiveness and extending conciliatory arms towards the widow of the murderer.

The families of those girls will never completely get over what has happened, yet the chances are that their faith, their incredibly supportive community, and their seemingly genuine desire not to harbour bitterness will give them strength to face the rest of life. Of course, it's not always like that; many people find it impossible to forgive, which actually makes it much harder for them in the long run. Unforgiveness, or a desire for revenge (not necessarily, I hasten to add, justice) can eat people up and certainly hinder any long-term healing process. More of that later.

When tragedies strike, like a bombing or an earthquake or a 9/11, the sense of communal loss and the marking of events with memorial services and so on seem to give people tremendous support. Actually, we need to remember that each person's loss is individual, and they still need to grieve on a very personal basis. I remember when my mother died some years ago thinking that the world should have stopped for a while. It didn't, though; everyone carried on as if nothing had happened, yet our family was grieving. We need to remember that trauma isn't just through accident or dramatic events; the loss of a loved one is always harrowing even when they may have been ill for some time.

Emotions and memories

When it comes to emotions, some people will quite happily revisit in their mind situations where they've been hurt, but many try to forget. Most of us will probably try to avoid going through similar situations to avoid pain, especially if we haven't resolved a particular issue. However, it's hard to tell how many people actually *suppress* memories. Sigmund Freud proposed that we all suppress unwanted and painful memories. The idea of unearthing these memories out of our unconscious mind became the basis of his psychoanalytical theory and techniques. Many people still assume that this is how all psychotherapy works; somehow discover the traumas of the past and allow them to come to your conscious mind and then you can deal with them. It's probably because Freud was the founder of the psychoanalytical school of psychology and the first name that comes to mind for most people that they make that assumption.

I must admit, when I first encountered a psychiatrist I hoped it would be that easy. Maybe he could put me into a relaxed state, not exactly under hypnosis maybe but nevertheless able to remember things without trying too hard. Perhaps I would be able to relive the time when my dad left; there could be things from my very early childhood that I'd suddenly remember and that in itself would cure me of any hang-ups I might have now. Alas, it wasn't to be that easy. The kind of therapy I was to undergo was not based on such practices. It was going to involve using my conscious mind a lot more than I realised.

Cognitive therapy, or cognitive behaviour therapy, is a kind of psychotherapy that many psychotherapists and counsellors use these days to treat a variety of problems, including depression and anxiety. It involves recognising unhelpful or destructive patterns of thinking and reacting, then modifying or replacing these with more realistic or helpful ones. The word cognitive comes from the Latin *cognoscere*, to know. In other words, the whole idea of therapy is to use your mind to understand, confront and in a sense begin to have control over the feelings or patterns of thought that are causing the problem. This will inevitably mean facing traumas, but it doesn't necessarily mean trying to remember every detail or even possibly looking for events that didn't actually happen. Sometimes people find it too hard to accept that the answers will come gradually from within them rather than through some dramatic revelation.

Please don't think that I'm dismissing the whole notion of suppressing memories. Statistics tell us that around a fifth of the population in the UK will be abused in some way at some time in their life. This could be sexual abuse, physical harm and/or bullying and there's no doubt that some might try to erase the memories of such awful things purely to survive, or it might be that they just couldn't understand what was going on because they were so young. Both society and the church are still only just waking up to the widespread nature of abuse. Thankfully, schools are much more aware of the problem of bullying and most try their utmost to deal with it. Sadly, it's something that is very hard sometimes to identify. Some people suffer in silence and are deeply scarred right into adult life. The same can be said of domestic abuse, and it's a cliché but oh so true when we say we don't know what goes on behind closed doors.

All kinds of feelings can burden people later in life, including a sense of guilt, uncleanness and/or a huge sense of unworthiness. These feelings need to be explored in an understanding and loving environment, and memories do need to be exposed if necessary. I'm simply saying we need to be balanced and pray for a huge amount of wisdom so that we don't overstate the case on the one hand nor ignore it on the other. We need to be open to the ability of the Holy Spirit to help people remember traumatic experiences, and to heal people of them by his power. However, I still want to emphasise the general importance of our adult minds understanding what's going on so that we eventually emerge much stronger.

Life Position

Parents, adults and children

After seeing a psychiatrist every week for a year and a half, both he and I felt the time had come to finish. The anxieties I'd been experiencing had subsided to the point where he was confident that I could cope with the process of understanding myself better. Certainly, I was free of the ideas I'd had of boxing things up and pretending it wasn't to do with the whole me, and of hoping that someone else could cure me with no effort on my part. It's true to say that nothing major had happened during the eighteen months to create the feeling of anger or anxiety at being left out again, so that test would still be to come.

I was left with a feeling that things were better, but I still wanted to know more about how some of these difficulties I'd had came about. I knew that we can never fully comprehend feelings, but as I said before understanding is important as far as we can have it. By this time I was married and had moved home. I had to visit a new GP about something else, but we were talking about my experiences. He recommended that I read a book that was proving very popular both here and in the United States. Indeed, Thomas Harris's *I'm OK – You're OK*[1] was a huge bestseller and communicated to a wide audience the whole technique called Transactional Analysis, or TA for short. Self-help groups had sprung up all over the place where people were using TA to help understand their emotions and why they acted as they did. I've already quoted from the book at the beginning of my chapter about understanding and healing.

It's important to remember that TA is only one type of cognitive therapy and I'm certainly not claiming it's the answer to everything. Some of it needs to be critiqued in the light of Scripture as well. However, much of what the book says made perfect sense to me and has helped me not only to understand my own mind but also to help others to an extent. I can only give a short description here and once again recommend that you read further if you want to know more.

The basis of TA is that we need to think of ourselves quite simply as divided into parent, adult and child. The adult is what it says; it's me now, with my adult mind that is able to reason, to see things in perspective, and that is adapted properly to current reality. The parent within me is a set of inherited feelings, attitudes and behaviour patterns that resemble those of a parent figure. They may be good or 'nurturing' feelings, or they may be prejudiced ones based on arbitrary values and prohibitive views. Everyone's adult tends to be affected or 'contaminated' by the parent to a greater or lesser extent. It's the function of the adult to understand this and evaluate what is helpful and what is not. Prejudice needs to be seen for what it is, for example, but this can only happen when in a sense we stand outside ourselves to make the evaluation.

It's the same when it comes to the child. The child is a set of feelings, attitudes and behaviour patterns that are left over from childhood. Again, the adult needs to recognise the child and separate out the attitudes and behaviour patterns, otherwise it remains controlled to a greater or lesser degree by the child. TA is all about understanding transactions between people. For example, someone strongly affected by the child might respond well to someone with strong parent characteristics. This needn't be a bad thing, but there are situations where it is not healthy. Sometimes people are relating adult to adult, but there may be an unexpected response from a person because their child has reacted to what they perceive as a parent in someone else (perhaps perceiving criticism when none actually exists).

OK about OK?

The real problem for most of us is that our adult is not entirely in control. The parent or the child, very often the latter in fact, is affecting us often more than we realise. The clue to see how we tick in all this is to understand our so-called 'life position', that is how we see ourselves in relation to everyone else in the world. I'll attempt to summarise the four life positions described by Harris, although as ever they can only be explained relatively briefly here and therefore inadequately. The argument is that everyone fits into one of these life positions.

I'm not OK – you're OK

To begin at the beginning, as they say. In the very early stages
of life an infant needs not only warmth and food, he (or she, of
course) also needs a lot of physical affection. The birth experience itself has been so unpleasant and the world around now
so threatening that repetitious bodily contact, summed up by
the word 'stroking', is actually essential to survival.

During the first two years of life the child does not have the
ability to put feelings into words, to build an explanation of
how he feels so uncertain in the world. Because the child's feelings and impressions of causality, that is 'what follows what',
are so uncertain and constantly changing, the child's primitive
perception of himself is that he's not really OK as a person. The
mother, or to an extent the father or anyone else providing
stroking, must be OK because they are the source of comfort.
To put it in Harris's own words:

> This is the universal position of early childhood, being the infant's
> logical conclusion from the situation of birth and infancy. There is
> OK-ness in this position, because stroking is present. Every child is
> stroked in the first year of life simply by the fact that he has to be
> picked up to be cared for. Without at least minimal handling the
> infant would not survive. There is also *not* OK-ness. That is the con-
> clusion about himself. I believe the evidence points to the over-
> whelming accumulation of *not* OK feelings in the child, making
> logical (on the basis of the evidence *he* has) his *not* OK conclusion
> about himself.[2]

In other words, the position that most of us adopt in the first
couple of years of life is that we are not really very 'all right'
people, where as everybody else around is. We haven't put this
actually into words because we can't, yet it's a position we have
adopted and unless anything happens to change this situation,
we will continue with this life position for the rest of our lives.
According to Harris, the vast majority of people adopt this life
position. Back to this in a minute.

I'm not OK – you're not OK

By the end of the first year of the child's life he can no longer rely on the same amount of stroking he had as a baby. If, however, at this stage there are no comforts at all, that is punishments are too hard or there is no comfort when he hurts himself, he may conclude that there is no hope of stroking from anyone. His view of his mother applies to all other people and he will end up rejecting their stroking and comfort. Needless to say this is not a happy situation at all.

I'm OK – you're not OK

Worse still is the situation for a child who is continually physically brutalised by his parents. The only way he can receive comfort for the pain he is feeling in his body is to be alone, away from the source of abuse. He is the one providing the 'stroking' for himself as he licks his wounds and he is the one who is OK, while others are not. He has survived, and must keep this life position to continue to survive. Apparently, many criminal psychopaths have adopted this position because of brutality in childhood. You can see why.

I'm OK – you're OK

Ideally, this is the life position that we should all have. This is where we truly believe that we're no better nor worse than anybody else. The world out there is OK, and everybody in it. I'm OK because I accept myself for who I am and I don't need stroking any more than anyone else. Harris believes that very few people achieve this position in childhood; rather they have to aim for it later on.

Conversion?

Apparently, when a life position is 'decided', all the things we experience in life we interpret selectively to support it. That's why, for example, many people see criticism when it's not really there. It's why some people think the Vicar has ignored them at the door of the church if he hasn't gone out of his way to make a fuss of them! If someone thinks they're not OK, they see everything in their world as supporting that view, and when it's extreme other people find it very difficult to handle them. Sometimes people avoid them, which of course perpetuates the whole thing.

As I read Harris's book all of this seemed to make perfect sense to me, but I wanted to make sure it squared up to what I believed as a Christian. In one sense, we're *not* all 'OK'. The Bible says we all come short of God's glory in our lives (Romans 3:23). The sinfulness and selfishness of our fallen nature mean that our hearts are not right with him (Psalm 14, Psalm 53:1, Jeremiah 17:9). I would refute any argument that this is simply born of some sort of self-hatred complex. To me it's a perfectly logical conclusion from observation that the human race has gone wrong and that human nature is such that we need forgiveness and help to be the holy people we are meant to be.

However, the Bible is also full of references to how much God loves us and to how much he is longing for us to return to him because we're precious. One of the most famous verses in the whole Bible tells us why Jesus came to die for us:

'For God so loved the world [that is, you and me] that he gave his one and only Son, that whoever believes in him shall not perish but have eternal life.' (John 3:16)

Psalm 139 even tells us that he knew us in the womb, and the Parable of the Prodigal Son shows us how deep the love of a heavenly Father goes in being prepared to accept us back into his presence (Luke 15).

As long as we have this balance in mind it seems to me quite legitimate to use the best of the various secular therapies to deal with a poor view of one's self. There have been many Christian books, sermons and seminars in recent years along the lines of how can we can't really love others properly if we can't learn firstly to love ourselves. I still maintain that understanding with the mind and allowing the Holy Spirit to work supernatural healing go together. With this particular therapy there is an act of the will, but I would ally it with submission to the Spirit. There is a decision to be made, which Harris even calls a 'conversion experience'.[3]

As I thought about my difficulties in the past I had begun to realise that it wasn't just about certain events that had so troubled me; it was about my general need to know I was an OK person, who didn't have to worry about being left out or whatever. I'm OK – you're OK was a *position* and not a feeling, and one that I could *choose* to adopt, as I identified the child in me for what it was. It didn't matter if I didn't have enough stroking at an early age, nor if my father leaving me at the age of eight was a punch in the emotional stomach; what mattered was that my adult held sway in the matter.

I suppose I had already begun to come to this conclusion previously, but understanding more about TA definitely pulled some of the threads together. At the same time, I believe it was also a matter of claiming the truth in my innermost being about God's boundless love for me. What's really amazing is how hard most of us find it to identify what's going on behind some of the irrational feelings we have, feelings that can lead to all sorts of emotional games we play with ourselves and others:

> In explaining Transactional Analysis to patients and non-patients I have found a generally *that's it!* response to the explanation of the origin and existence of the *not* OK child.[4]

That's really how I felt, so too have most of the people I've come across who have grasped the concept.

When you think about it, it's amazing how we survive past early childhood really. An infant who can't put into words what he sees, hears and experiences is probably more likely to feel bad about himself than the opposite. If his parents argue a lot, for example, he can't exactly rationalise along the lines,

'Oh, Mummy and Daddy are having a row. Grownups do this from time to time. They really ought to get over it. Anyway, it's nothing to do with me.' The usual feeling, unfounded though it is, is that it's somehow his fault because he hasn't learned yet that he isn't the centre of the universe. He thinks everything must relate to him. The feeling can't be verbalised so it's internalised and contributes to the life position where he's quite simply not OK. The question most of us have to ask ourselves is do we want to carry on feeling not OK, or do we want to grasp the opportunity to change?

Sin/Curses/Demonisation

A spiritual matter

This is the last major category I want to look at in considering what makes us the people we are. This could easily be three major sections on their own and many books have been written about each, although they overlap and intertwine considerably. I want to think about them together relatively briefly in order simply to remind us that inner healing isn't just about the mind, the emotions or social and human factors. Ultimately, wholeness of being is a spiritual matter, and as such it goes far deeper than any of those things. I have realised in my own journey of healing how much I need to remember that it all begins not with me alone but with my relationship with my Creator.

We've just been looking at a whole therapy based on making people feel better about themselves, and now here we are about to consider a subject that could have the opposite effect! This need not be the case, as long as we have a proper understanding of forgiveness, healing and deliverance. It's important to remember that whatever we say about these things, the Lord's desire is to set people free because he loves them and because he wants them to experience more of his love. I hope that nothing I say will make anyone feel guilty or condemned in any way, quite the opposite. Whatever the relevance of any of this is to each of us, let's all remember the Scripture, '. . . there is now *no condemnation* for those who are in Christ Jesus' (Romans 8:1).

The sins of the fathers

Earlier we looked at how the past can affect us now. If we believe this is a fallen world then we have to acknowledge that there is a basic flaw in human nature and each generation inherits the consequences of humankind's sin. Even if we don't believe in all that, sheer honesty would surely make us admit that there is a lot wrong with the human race. We just don't seem to learn from the past, nor are we as free from its influences as many people would like to think.

One of the verses of Scripture that some Christian writers and preachers have made a lot of is Exodus 20:5 . . .'. . . for I, the Lord your God, am a jealous God, punishing the children for the sin of the fathers to the third and fourth generation of those who hate me'.

When we take passages from the Old Testament we have to be discerning about whether words were meant in a particular way within the context, or whether they were meant to be taken as general principles. For example, most of us would agree that the Ten Commandments are basic precepts for all. Hence murder, adultery and so on are wrong for everyone.

However, many of the laws given to the Israelites were to do with the worship and way of life that they were to adhere to in order to maintain their unique identity in the midst of all the pagan tribes around. We need to ask if the idea of punishing subsequent generations for the sins of their forebears, for which the descendants were not themselves directly responsible, is part of maintaining that uniqueness. On the other hand, is it a general principle for everyone?

This is an argument that may never be resolved. However, it's probably fair to conclude that the sin of one generation may well have an effect years later. Some of the things we mentioned earlier, the treatment of the Welsh, the Irish or the

American Indians for example, were obviously to do with sinfulness even if it wasn't seen like that by both sides at the time. The effects have been long-lasting, and it's precisely because sin was involved that acts of forgiveness and reconciliation have been so important for long-term healing.

What about 'generational sin' when it comes to families? The problem here is that not many of us can trace our ancestry in the necessary detail. I have no idea if there was ever some blatant act of rebellion against God, or a serious crime, or sinfulness, or cruelty, on either side of my family way back. I can of course look at my parents' breakup and say that sin was the basic cause. If that's the case, God *has* broken in and dealt with the consequences, bringing so much healing to me.

It's all a question of balance. I have no doubt it's right to use whatever information we can about the past, but equally it can't be right to dwell on it too much. After all, walking with Jesus is about acknowledging his power breaking into your life from the day you decide to follow him. It's also about walking forwards into the future and not looking back. And if God is a god of judgment, he is also merciful. Even if Exodus 20:5 is true for all of us, we shouldn't forget the next verse which completes the sentence: '. . . but showing love to a thousand [generations] of those who love me and keep my commandments'.

Personal sin

Other Old Testament passages could be quoted referring to this wonderful balance between the righteous anger and extensive mercy of God. In the end, far more important than dwelling on the sins of the fathers is the fact that we each bear personal responsibility for our actions: 'Fathers shall not be put to death for their children, nor children put to death for their fathers; each is to die for his own sin' (Deuteronomy 24:16).

That's pretty clear isn't it? God's priorities lie ultimately in his relationship with each one of us. As we've seen, he knows us better than we know ourselves. Just as Jesus knew what was in the hearts of the religious leaders when they kept getting things wrong, so he knows our failings as well as the things that have conspired against us in life.

This talk about sin is at odds with much secular therapy when talking about the human condition. That's because it's not simply describing people as victims, but as creatures with responsibility. Actually, I don't believe there's a conflict at all; it's simply a question, as I said earlier, of taking that which is good within secular understanding and using it within the context of what the Bible tells us about ourselves. Much that happened to me earlier in my life was not my fault; I have no problems in saying that. But it doesn't take away from the fact that I need to repent if any of my emotional reactions have come from an element of self-absorption. I'll come back to this theme later on.

Unforgiveness

It seems to me that they were two particular sins at the top of Jesus' list. One was out and out hypocrisy, where people made an outward display of religion without having any real love for God. Many of the religious leaders failed to understand what a relationship with him was all about, and fell into the trap of legalism as they tried to keep all the rules and regulations of their religion without having any real faith themselves.

The other sin that Jesus mentioned on several occasions was that of *unforgiveness*. Many times he tried to explain that we cannot experience the liberating forgiveness of our heavenly Father unless we can forgive others. And if we can't experience the forgiveness of the Father then we can't be truly free to develop as human beings.

In the New Testament there are two main Greek words used meaning 'to forgive'. One of them, *charizomai*, is to do with bestowing favour unconditionally (as the believers are exhorted to do in Ephesians 4:32). The more common one, *aphiemi*, literally means to let go, to send away, to dismiss, or to cancel a debt. It's there for example in the Lord's Prayer (Matthew 6:12, 14–15) where we are to ask the Father to forgive us *as we* forgive others. It's there where Jesus declares a paralysed man forgiven (Matthew 9:2).

The whole idea of letting go is so important, because if we can't forgive someone then in our minds we are trying to enslave them. The reality is, we are the ones who are enslaved. So many people are bound up and affected in some way psychologically and spiritually because they can't 'let go' of someone. In Luke 6:37 Jesus uses yet another word, *apoluo*, when he says quite plainly, 'Forgive, and you will be forgiven.' He's literally saying, 'Let loose and you will be let loose.' Don't we want to be free in this way? I'm really glad I had the opportunity to tell my father that I forgave him, although I'm not entirely sure that was the whole issue for me in the long run. I think in a sense I had to learn to let go and forgive *all* those involved who perhaps had ended up making me feel left out and insignificant. Of course, it wasn't their fault and there was no logic to any of it, but I had been bound up all the same.

What is a curse?

> See, I am setting before you today a blessing and a curse – the blessing if you obey the commands of the LORD your God that I am giving you today; the curse if you disobey the commands of the LORD your God and turn from the way that I command you today by following other gods, which you have not known. (Deuteronomy 11:26–28)

We generally think of a curse as something that is put on somebody else in a malevolent way. When God talked about a curse coming upon the Israelites if they disobeyed him, he was of course talking about the consequences of stepping outside his blessing. Blessing was quite simply the opposite of cursing. In a very real way, if we sin against him then we too are outside his blessing and have to accept what that might lead to, given that there are many influences all around us, both physical and spiritual.

The Jews believed that when somebody spoke out a word, it took on a very tangible form. Therefore, if somebody pronounced a blessing on a person or a place they believed that there would be very real benefits. A curse uttered would also have very real effects, although of course detrimental ones. Any sort of negative word against someone was a serious business. Jesus didn't mince his words about what would happen to the man who called his brother a fool (Matthew 5:22).

The fact is that curses were pronounced, even by seemingly righteous people such as the prophets. Even God, as we see, can pronounce a curse. So how will we define what it means to curse someone? We might summarise it as speaking out that which is basically negative. If someone says, 'Nothing good ever happens to me,' they're effectively pronouncing a sort of curse on themselves. If a child is told that they're useless, that's a kind of curse. The point is, these utterances will have an effect that can be deep and longlasting.

If this broad definition is accurate, then it means far more of us than we might think may have been at some point the objects of cursing. Of course, this doesn't preclude the more obvious sort of curse that could be put on a person or even on a family and a family-line. This might include a gypsy curse, or one pronounced by someone with a vendetta. We need to be aware of these and, as we'll see in a minute, not forget that there is such a thing as evil.

Dealing with them

How shall we deal with curses? Sometimes it might be right to show our disdain for a so-called curse. I've heard of how missionaries have had curse symbols placed on their houses and then deliberately hung them up in a prominent position to show that they're not afraid of them. This sort of thing might not happen very much to most of us, but we do need to show as Christians that we don't walk in the kind of superstitious dread that some people do. At other times, if we know about some untoward attack involving a curse, such as a word spoken deliberately against us or our family, it can be a good idea to pray with someone about it. That someone could be a Christian friend, or of course a minister or church leader who is understanding about this kind of thing.

It's important to remember that the power of God is infinitely greater than the power behind any curse. We don't want to be praying with any doubt about that, nor with any degree of fear. As long as we're in a right relationship with the Lord we can rest in his love for us, since 'perfect love drives out fear' (1 John 4:18). We always need to pray in the name of Jesus, because his name alone has the authority against such things. Indeed, our prayer might take the form of a rebuke against the curse and what lies behind it. We need to learn to use the authority given to us as children of God.

Much of the time it will be a question of confronting more generally negative words that have had an adverse effect upon us over the years. Again, if we know about these we can bring them to the Lord and 'come against them' in the name of Jesus. If we're not aware of specific things, it might still be right if we've never done so before to invite the Lord in a general way to deal with anything negative in our lives. There's not a lot of point in dwelling on all this, nor of trying to remember things that may not be there in the first place.

In the end, the best way to deal with the negative is to accentuate the positive! The children of Israel had a choice, to follow the way of cursing or to walk the way of blessing. However we deal with curses or the potential of them in our lives, we need someone (it could be ourselves or someone else) to pronounce the Lord's blessing upon us. As long as we don't live lives that involve deliberate ongoing sin we should have an attitude of expectation that we can walk in that blessing. I'm sure that will include our mental state, indeed our whole person if we allow it.

Warfare

'The supreme activity of the devil is upon the mind of man'.[5]

Anyone who has tried to follow Christ for a length of time will be aware of what a battle they are in. So often you can find yourself struggling to do what you know is right, but often failing and being left with a sense of your own sin. It wasn't like that before you became a Christian! The Bible is very clear that ultimately we're not fighting against flesh and blood, including our own, but against 'the spiritual forces of evil in the heavenly realms' (Ephesians 6:12). Jesus believed in the existence of Satan, and a significant part of his ministry included the setting free of those who were demonised.

As with the whole subject of cursing, it's very important that we maintain a sense of balance in the whole subject of spiritual warfare. Christians have taken various extreme stances over the years. On the one hand, they attribute almost everything bad to demonic activity. All kinds of methods of dealing with it have sprung up, including various counselling techniques. One of the most controversial of these approaches was that of Dr Kenneth McAll. He believed that even our family trees needed 'healing' because we could be influenced in our mental state by certain of our ancestors having been possessed by evil spirits. In some way we're still under the control of these spirits.

The other extreme is when we dismiss the existence of the demonic completely and put everything concerning mental disorder or malaise down to human factors. In our society we do seem to have lost touch with the whole notion of the supernatural, thinking that science and rationality explain all. Actually, it's interesting that people are turning away from this and seeking once again the spiritual. The problem is, they can end up more superstitious than in the past if God and his revealed truth in the Word are left out of the picture.

Personally, I think the truth lies somewhere between the two extremes. I do believe that it is possible for somebody to be 'possessed' by an evil spirit or spirits. I have no doubt of the existence of these, apparently being angelic beings who were cast out of the presence of God along with Satan himself. However, we shouldn't credit the devil and his minions with more power than they have. They are nothing like as powerful as God himself, and the name of Jesus has complete authority over them. Nor should we go looking for a demon in every corner.

The fact is that most of us will come across demon possession (or to translate it more accurately, 'demonisation') relatively rarely. My opinion is that we shouldn't seek to be involved in deliverance ministry, only to be aware that we might come across the need, especially these days as people enter the Kingdom of God from a society which is increasingly pagan. Most of the time, the evil we have to deal with is in our personal lives, where we struggle against temptation.

Even here, we have to be careful not to attribute too much to Satan. Unlike God, he cannot be everywhere at once. It follows therefore that most of the time our temptations will be in fact struggles with our own flesh, or 'self'. That doesn't rule out engagement with the enemy and taking authority against him when we pray. My experience is that when someone says or thinks they're 'possessed by an evil spirit', then the likelihood is they're not. Most people that are in any way demonised are usually unaware of the fact until the Holy Spirit reveals it in prayer and/or counselling. We need to keep level-headed in the whole business.

The love of God

If we do get involved in deliverance ministry we need to remember that this is all about bringing the love of God into someone's life. We are not out to condemn anyone. Traditionally, teachers on this subject have spoken about how it is possible to give 'footholds' for the enemy. I have no doubt this is true, and we need to remember that the human mind can be influenced very easily, especially if it is not in control. That's why being blind drunk or heavily under the influence of drugs can lay people open to the demonic.

I've no doubt that deliberate and ongoing sinfulness of a certain kind can lay people open also. However, if we read the Bible carefully we actually see demonised people as victims towards whom Jesus showed tremendous compassion. I'd like to quote if I may from a commentary on Luke's Gospel by Norval Geldenuys, which is most interesting:

> It is noteworthy that Jesus nowhere speaks of forgiveness of sins or of purification-sacrifices that have to be brought after His hearing of such cases (as He did in some cases of physical illness). Those possessed are depicted throughout as unfortunate sufferers who by no fault of their own are dominated by evil spirits and who, when the spirits are cast out by Jesus, accept their deliverance with joy and gratitude (Mark 5:18–20, Luke 8:2).[6]

Somehow we keep coming back to the subject of God's love. In all my struggles with emotions and anxieties I was so glad that this was the one thing I could rely on. It's what really kept me going, to know that he didn't condemn me even if I didn't think very highly of myself. I have no doubt that the devil wanted to work on my guilt at not being emotionally 'together' as a Christian.

In praying with other Christians I tried to make sure that most things were covered. For example, I did know that my maternal grandfather, I think having a struggle with the Christian faith, had at some point visited a spiritualist. I know that when I was taking O levels he asked this person to pray for me, although to whom or what they prayed I have no idea. I don't know if this really influenced my life in any way, but just to be sure the whole episode was covered with prayer and the Lord invited to deal with anything as necessary.

In the end, we're talking here about being sensible. Let's be open to the possibilities of how evil might affect us, but let's also be realistic about what comes from within. In all this we really need two things; common sense and the Holy Spirit gift of discernment. As Mark Stibbe says:

> This is a gift which we therefore need to desire. It is not a fashionable gift, like prophecy or healing. But it is necessary and a vital gift. . . . Handled wisely and well, this particular ability could well prove to be one of the most priceless gifts in the years that lie ahead. May the Lord grant us more discerning people in his Church.[7]

May he do so indeed!

Wonderful people

And so we come to the end of my attempted roundup of some of the many factors that might go to 'make me me'. I know it's by no means exhaustive and you can probably think of others. We're all different, and not everyone will relate to everything I've been talking about. If we genuinely don't think a particular influence is relevant to us, then we shouldn't spend undue time dwelling on it. However, as I said before, let's remember just how complicated we human beings are. We are indeed 'fearfully and wonderfully made'.

Because of that, it's easy for things to go wrong and all I'm asking is that we should step back from ourselves and ask God to show us something of how we came to be what we are. If in doing so he reveals something to us, then we should be honest and seek help if necessary. At the same time, let's rejoice and celebrate that we are such wonderful creatures, the pinnacle of his creation and of the pouring out of his love. As I return now to telling my story, I hope you'll see that what I've been trying to talk about in the last few chapters isn't theory, but part of my own discovery of how much I'm worth as a human being.

Notes

1. Thomas Harris, *I'm OK – You're OK*, (Arrow Books, orig. publ. 1967).

2. *Ibid*, p. 42.
3. *Ibid*, p. 49.
4. *Ibid*, p. 42.
5. D.M. Lloyd-Jones, *The Christian Warfare*, (Banner of Truth Trust, 1976, p. 85).
6. Norval Geldenuys, *The Gospel of Luke*, (New London Commentaries series, Marshal, Morgan and Scott, 1951, p. 174).
7. Mark Stibbe, *Know Your Spiritual Gifts*, (Marshal Pickering, 1997, p. 150).

CHAPTER TEN

THE NEW SHOES GLOW

Selection

After waiting the two years I'd been asked to, I went forward again to explore the possibility of ordination training. There was a new Director of Ordinands in post who was very positive and eventually I was put forward for a selection conference. I knew that at some point I would need to talk about the problems I'd had in the past. Before my selection conference I was asked to have a medical, which actually involved simply speaking to a doctor in London, presumably to make sure I wasn't likely to go off the rails. The three-day conference itself, as anyone who has been on one will tell you, was a pretty intense affair with several individual interviews, observed group discussions, written exercises, and so on. Most people find it hard to relax at these things, some finding it harder going than others. I didn't find it particularly helpful to have a nearby church clock chiming every quarter of an hour throughout the night! Nevertheless, I survived the experience and a few days later received a letter from my bishop saying I had been accepted for ordination training.

I can honestly say that had the Advisory Council for the Church's Ministry (ACCM) turned me down it would not have been the end of the world. Of course it was something I wanted on one level, although I still found it very hard to imagine myself as a vicar. Deep down I knew that God had a plan for my life. If

I had been turned down I probably would have had to train for something else, possibly teaching. I certainly couldn't have carried on in the job I was. But I can honestly say that I didn't see ordination as a prize to be gained at all costs and I would have accepted not getting through as God's will. Sometimes I wonder if on one level I wouldn't have been a little relieved!

Anyway, a whole new horizon opened up for Jane and me. For various reasons we put off my going to college for another year. For one thing, Jane was studying for professional insurance exams at the time. Also, we had bought a house and wanted to be in it for a while at least, and we felt we still had a job to do at St. John's. In spite of the struggle I had with my job, we felt the Lord telling us to wait a bit longer. The timing turned out to be perfect. Jane needed to carry on working as the church grant I was going to get would not support her as well as me. When we eventually went to our college of choice, Trinity College in Bristol, she managed to get a transfer doing exactly the same job as she had been doing in Birmingham. She had worked in a specialised type of insurance, namely haulage, and the sub company she worked for only had two people working in Bristol. The woman doing her equivalent job left to have a baby at just the right time for us. Jane was able to slot in for the two years we were in Bristol without having to learn a new job. God is so good.

We had looked at a couple of theological colleges and decided on Trinity for various reasons. The course I was to do was similar to anywhere else, but there did seem to be a sense of openness to the Holy Spirit within an intellectual environment, and above all a real family atmosphere. The Principal, George Carey, made us very welcome. I was to be in his tutor group during my time at college, never imagining that he would be my bishop for a while one day, and then go on to be Archbishop of Canterbury.

A test

When I filled in the forms for college I remember a question that asked if you had had any mental illness in the last five years. The truth was I hadn't, as it had been some time since my problems. In any case ACCM had known all about it. I was really looking forward to this new direction in life, and particularly to getting away to another city especially as I had attended university without doing that. The whole thing was quite scary I suppose, but very exciting at the same time. I was really glad that not only had I resolved so many emotional issues in the past, but I had also been able to discuss these quite freely in order to move on with this new phase of my life. I wasn't quite prepared for this to be tested just before going away to train, but something happened to do just that.

During the early part of the summer of 1984 before we went to college, Jane was called on to do jury service in the Crown Court. Normally, for most people this wouldn't be a very big deal, simply an inconvenience. However, I suddenly felt the same feelings that I had felt before. Of course I wasn't allowed to know details, but I knew enough about the nature of one of the cases she served on for it to bring out both rational and irrational feelings in me. I would still say that the rational feelings, those of a natural protectiveness of a man towards his wife, were quite founded. As it happens, I had to learn to live with that. The real issue was dealing with the irrational feelings.

It was something I was determined to sort out in my own mind and, hopefully, before I went to college. Looking back, perhaps I should have shared it more freely with someone such as my vicar. I suppose the problem was I didn't want to have to go over everything again with another person. I'm not sure that I was that good at hiding my feelings, even though I tried, and 'going it alone' may not have been the best thing. I do believe in sharing a problem with the right people for prayer and healing. Indeed, it's normally vital in a church context that we operate truly as a body that cares for its members. However, it was particularly important for me to know that I could find the understanding within me in order to allow God to do his work once again.

It took me quite a while to understand why this happened when it did, but I think I know that it was a pretty good test. At least I was able to carry on more or less with normal life, including going to work. I'm glad to say that it didn't spoil the whole adventure of going to college at all, and the next two years would prove a very happy time. What it did do was further crystallise some of the things I had learned about myself and certainly take this learning out of the realms of theory.

New shoes

Earlier, I tried to put into words what my emotional difficulties had been in the past. Originally I wondered if I had felt a kind of misdirected protectiveness towards Jane whenever she took part in an activity at which I couldn't be present. I had come to realise that this was not the case, and that the feelings were a kind of anger or resentment at not being able to have similar experiences myself. That's because I somehow saw such experiences as the kind that make somebody important, albeit temporarily. It meant that I wanted something to happen to me, not necessarily the same thing but at least something similarly 'out of the ordinary'. If that something couldn't happen, I was left simply with unresolved jealousy or the desire for the experience not to happen to someone else. I had come to realise that this was all to do with my longing to feel important inside.

Everybody needs to feel important, in the right sense of the word. We all need to know that we're special. How will this come? It might be about the baby that is stroked sufficiently, or the toddler who is made to feel good by the praises of their parents, or other factors. If the whole 'I'm not OK' syndrome I described earlier is true, then most of us grow up with at least some degree of feeling bad about ourselves. Our self-image might be poor, we might have the old 'inferiority complex' which nothing will dispel because we're totally convinced of it. Or it might be that we just don't feel important enough. Perhaps we didn't get enough affirmation at particularly vulnerable stages in our life.

For me it might have been early on or, as I've suggested is probably the case, it was at that vulnerable period of parental break up. That was certainly a time when I felt left out, feeling insignificant and 'small', and worse still probably blaming myself for what happened to my parents. Ever since, I'd needed desperately to have attention, to be made to feel important again.

Do you remember what it was like to be taken into a shop when you were a child to be fitted for a new pair of shoes? I'll always remember the 'glow' I felt in me. For those few minutes I was the centre of the universe. I was so important and it made me feel tremendously good about myself. Someone was paying me exclusive attention, just for a brief period. This 'new shoes glow' is something everyone probably experiences from time to time, even if it doesn't last. Maybe you can relate it to something else. As older human beings we might experience it in other, sometimes subtler, ways. Perhaps it's the attention from a lover, or even when people sing 'Happy Birthday' to us! I think if we're honest most of us enjoy attention, we just don't always want to admit it.

I think it has to be that if we have enough of this when we're young, we are less likely to crave it when we're older; we'll pass better into the 'I'm OK' state. Thomas Harris says that most of us don't actually achieve this, but surely it has to be a question of degree. For some reason, I must have been left with a tremendously unfulfilled need. I believed in my head that I was a child of God; I knew he loved me but somehow that still wasn't enough to make me feel the special child I actually was.

I'm sure that many of us have the same feelings to a greater or lesser degree, but they will manifest themselves in different ways. Munchausen Syndrome is an extreme example, where someone feigns a disease, an illness, or a psychological trauma and might even be prepared to take all sorts of risks in order to draw attention or sympathy to themselves. Then there are people who might practise self-harm or resort to attempted suicide, or maybe talk about suicide as a cry for attention. Eating disorders may well fit in somewhere along the spectrum in talking about the need for attention, although there is still much research going on into the causes of the various disorders.

For others, this basic need for attention may reveal itself in a variety of other less dramatic activities. For many people, as it was for me, they might simply find themselves being envious of other people. In my case it was simply that I was feeling this very forcibly inside.

Jealousy

Is there a difference between envy and jealousy? Well, I suppose jealousy can have its redeeming side. It's possible to be jealous in a protective sense, such as when God himself wishes to keep the special relationship he has with Israel (e.g. Exodus 20:5, 34:14). Usually, though, jealousy and envy are closely inter-twined. Envy is when we wish we had something that someone else has; somehow what they have, whether a material posses-sion or a talent or a particular experience, increases them and diminishes us. Jealousy takes the whole thing further. It might involve relationships; it certainly involves deep emotions (the word originally comes from the Latin and Greek words for 'zeal'). We basically *want* what another person or other people have and we can be deeply unhappy if we can't have it.

The experience I had before going to college served to empha-sise those deep underlying feelings that were obviously still part of my makeup. The only reason I felt what I did so strongly was because it involved the person closest to me. The fact is, I could still feel jealousy towards other people if deep down I per-ceived that what they had and I didn't made me not such a worthwhile person. It might be felt to a lesser extent with those people than with my wife but nevertheless it was still real.

The only reason I can really talk about all this is because I believe it to be an incredibly common human experience. I had the problem quite badly, yet it took me a long time to identify it. I believe many others suffer similarly, but fail to identify it. It might not be as strong as it was in me, but it's still there. I really do believe it was important for me to have had these things sorted out before going to theological college. I'm convinced that it can be a problem amongst church leaders as much as anyone and not to have identified it in myself would have caused untold problems in future ministry.

Our problem as Christians is that jealousy is ultimately a sin and therefore to admit to it is far too difficult, even to ourselves let alone to others. Sometimes that's even worse for church leaders. Jealousy might be a sin, but it's no worse than any other, and as with all sin we need to try to understand what causes it.

If you don't believe me about how common jealousy is, simply take a look at the Bible. When I did a brief survey I was amazed how often the theme crops up. Consider the following examples:

- Satan against God. Apparently Satan was created with so much of the beauty of God in him. We know little about his origins, but his desire to destroy mankind and all the works of God seem to be born of an aspiration to take God's place. Does that show a fundamental jealousy? Traditionally many have thought that Isaiah 14:12ff, while ostensibly referring to the King of Babylon, also refers to Satan . . .

   How you have fallen from heaven, O morning star (AV *Lucifer*), son of the dawn! You have been cast down to the earth, you who once laid low the nations! You said in your heart, 'I will ascend to heaven; I will raise my throne above the stars of God . . .'

- Adam and Eve (Genesis 3). The basic sin was disobedience, but didn't a desire to be like God (v. 5) also involve wanting something he had and they didn't?
- Cain against Abel (Genesis 4). Murder as the result of jealousy.
- Hagar and Sarai (Genesis 16 and 21).
- Jacob and Esau (Genesis 27).
- Rachel and Leah (Genesis 29 and 30).
- Joseph's brothers against him (Genesis 37).
- Miriam and Aaron against Moses (Numbers 12).

- Korah and other leaders against Moses (Numbers 16).
- King Saul against David (1 Samuel 18).
- Absalom against King David (2 Samuel 13–18).
- The 'enemies of Judah and Benjamin' against Ezra and the people of Jerusalem (Ezra 4).
- Sanballat, Tobiah and others against Nehemiah and the people of Jerusalem (Nehemiah 4).
- Haman against Mordecai (Esther 6).
- Herod against the baby Jesus (Matthew 2).
- The religious leaders against Jesus (Matthew 27:18).
- The disciples amongst themselves? (Matthew 18:1).
- The older brother against the prodigal son (Luke 15:28–30). A fictional parable, but obviously an important detail to Jesus.
- Simon the Sorcerer against Peter and John (Acts 8: 9–24).
- The religious leaders against the apostles (Acts 5:17, 13:44).
- False teachers and 'super apostles' against Paul and other church leaders (Philippians 1:15, 2 Corinthians 11:5).

Insecurity

These are just a few examples where we have jealousy specifically mentioned or hinted at. I'm sure many of the rivalries between the ruling families of Judah and Israel also involved strong feelings of jealousy. Obviously, every situation will have been different in some way and it's impossible for us to know all that was going on in people's minds. Just occasionally, we get a glimpse of what's behind the actions of an individual.

Take Absalom, the son of King David, for example. His need for the power of the throne apparently has its roots in his relationship with his father. Absalom is banished from the King's presence after killing Amnon in revenge for the rape of his sister Tamar. Although the story says that David 'longed to go to Absalom', there doesn't seem to be any real understanding or expression of feeling between them when they are finally reconciled. After two years separation, there's no real sense that Absalom feels accepted by his father. The most likely explanation is that deep down he has a very poor self-image, having failed in his eyes to win the approval of his father. The damage had been done. It's hardly surprising that jealousy would be the result of such insecurity. Absalom ends up trying to seize the throne of Israel, and the whole thing ends tragically in his death and huge remorse on David's part.

Probably most of us are aware of how destructive envy and jealousy can be. No wonder the Bible has so much to say about it. Here are just some examples:

A heart at peace gives life to the body, but envy rots the bones. (Proverbs 14:30)

And I saw that all labour and all achievement spring from man's envy of his neighbour. This too is meaningless, a chasing after the wind. (Ecclesiastes 4:4)

Let us behave decently, as in the daytime, not in orgies and drunkenness, not in sexual immorality and debauchery, not in dissension and jealousy. (Romans 13:13)

For where you have envy and selfish ambition, there you find disorder and every evil practice. (James 3:16)

If the Bible has so much to say about the subject, then we really should take it seriously. Every one of us needs to examine our heart, to ask the Holy Spirit to reveal to us any jealousies we might be harbouring without even realising it. We need to question whether we might be feeling what we feel out of insecurity, because we actually have a poor self-image and still need something to give us importance emotionally.

Leadership

I'm convinced this is something we need to take seriously in the whole realm of church leadership. Here, once again, there is a need for balance. I'm sure that there's no problem in having a healthy kind of ambition to see a church grow. Jesus commanded us to go into the world and make disciples of all peoples. He has chosen to use the church, his body here on earth, as the vehicle through which people might be saved and enter his Kingdom. If you believe that people's personal salvation is important, then you know we need to see as many people as possible becoming Christians. Logically, that means that local churches need to grow in numbers, although ideally with new Christians and not with those transferred from other church fellowships.

If this is 'success', then may all churches and church leaders be successful! The problem is, there is often a tendency to cast an eye in the direction of other churches. Do they really have that many people on a Sunday morning in church? Is their Sunday School really that big? Why haven't we got a youth group as thriving as theirs? How come we can't seem to raise as much money as they do? And so on. Rather than being secure in our calling both as children of God and leaders with a specific job to do, many of us if we're honest tend to compare ourselves with others. 'Success' means then becoming bigger and better than anyone else's church around, rather than simply achieving what God has given you to do.

The fact is that not all church fellowships will grow into huge ones. Sometimes, people are working in difficult situations where much of their ministry is about sowing seeds rather than seeing a great harvest. Jesus reminded us that many seeds will fall onto ground that will not bear fruit. There will always be the 'hard places' for the Gospel. This might be in a rural or inner-city situation where resources are limited and natural leaders are few. God is looking for leaders in these places who are faithful in their witness and ministry. That's not an excuse for decline, however. I believe that any church that is open to renewal in the Holy Spirit is capable of growing. It can happen, even in the 'unfashionable' places. In the end, Jesus told us to pray for a reaping of the harvest that is ready (Matthew 9:38).

I may be wrong, but I think an unhealthy rivalry can be worse sometimes amongst male primary church leaders. Many are so-called 'alpha males' by nature. Alpha males are born leaders; they're usually quick-witted, assertive, self-confident and sometimes aggressive. Apparently women can have alpha traits also, but tend to empathise with people better rather than confronting or intimidating them.[1] I'd like to think that male church leaders have some female qualities, but if I'm honest the reality is that very often we don't. It can make us volatile and unwilling to be patient with those who are not like us. Above all, it can make us competitive. In itself, especially in commerce and industry, such a characteristic can be helpful. In church life, it can be destructive. It can also mean that leaders are very vulnerable. If they don't think they're being successful, or indeed if they're not getting enough positive feedback (or even praise), they can either become extremely jealous of other leaders, or become disillusioned and depressed.

Of course, this is a generalisation and not every male leader will be how I've just described. Nevertheless, I'm sure we need a lot more honesty amongst us sometimes. It's too easy to play games, where our conversations operate on one level but underneath there are conflict, rivalry and a lot of potentially confusing emotions. Such things might be present in leadership at other levels in church life as well as the primary ones, and we all need to be more aware of the dynamics involved.

Into the fray

I thoroughly enjoyed my time at Trinity. Looking back, it would have been nice to do a third year and come out with a theology degree as well as continuing to enjoy the close fellowship with people in the same boat. I was over the age of thirty when I went to college and was therefore only allowed to do a diploma for two years. As it happens, I was quite impatient to get stuck in to what I felt called to do. Jane and I returned to Birmingham to 'serve my title' (that is, to train as a curate before taking charge of my own church). I was enormously blessed to serve under the relatively new Rector of Christ Church The Quinton, on the west side of Birmingham bordering the Black Country. He had been one of the curates at St. John's Harborne and we had become great friends. Some people queried whether working with someone we knew so well would be a good thing. I believe we managed to maintain an excellent balance between friendship and a professional relationship.

What was exciting about ministering in that particular church was that there was much work to be done in terms of bringing renewal in the Holy Spirit. The church had had a liberal theological history, the legacy of which was quite marked. There was a strong resistance to change, not that that's unusual in a church. It was also a very large parish with just two full-time leaders to cover an enormous number of baptisms, weddings and funerals. I learned a lot, not only in the day-to-day stuff of church life, but also in handling change, opposition and introducing new styles of worship while allowing space for the Spirit to move in peoples lives.

Our first two children were born while we were in Quinton. When you consider all the attention an expectant mother gets, I suppose you could say it was a good test of whether I was free of the emotional upheaval of past years. Actually, I can think of much better ways of getting attention than pregnancy and childbirth! All in all, our four years in that place were excellent preparation for what lay ahead. I learned much about ordained ministry and despite the busyness we had space to bring up two young children.

Over the years I think I've learned never to say 'never' to God. Originally, I hadn't wanted to be a Church of England clergyman for reasons I've explained, but God had other ideas. When it was time to look for my first 'living' (that is, in a church where I would be the primary leader) I remember filling in the form necessary for my details to be circulated to bishops across the country. Jane and I were quite sure that we would never want to be in rural ministry, nor would we want to live in the southeast of England. The last few years have seen us live both in the countryside and east of London!

At the time, no real opportunities were appearing for me to serve in parishes in the Birmingham Diocese. Jane suggested I write to George Carey, who had not long been appointed as Bishop of Bath and Wells. I didn't like the thought of preferential treatment, just because I'd been a student of his, but it did seem logical at least to write to see if there were any vacancies. To my surprise very soon one appeared, but whereas I had hoped it might be in one of the larger towns in Somerset it turned out to be a rural benefice of two parishes right in the southeast corner of the county, nearly in Dorset.

Uncharted territory

Ordination is a big step in anyone's life. In the evangelical wing of the church the belief is that we are all priests and can all have a priestly ministry in the kingdom of God. Unfortunately, we still manage to put ordained church leaders on a pedestal. On one level, we believe that all Christians are equal, but on another level we think that vicars and ministers are a breed apart. Whether we think it's right or not, it can put an awful lot of pressure on those who are ordained.

However, I have to say that in terms of stepping out and taking responsibility, working first in a curacy (as is the practice in the Church of England) still shields you from the realities of taking on a primary leadership role. In all honesty, nothing could have prepared me for running two country parishes. I felt 'ready' in terms of my calling from the Lord, and in time being secure in that calling proved to be the most important thing. In terms of details, it was a question of learning as I went along. There wasn't a lot of administrative help available to me, although the church-wardens of both parishes were very helpful and supportive.

It meant learning about things I hadn't encountered in my curacy; being a governor at two church schools, preparing

sermons for most Sundays of the year, administering a churchyard, dealing with an architect over repairs to mediaeval build-
ings, administering ancient charities (one of which needed a
huge amount of paperwork done after an audit by the Charity
Commission), understanding about the needs of the farming community, dealing with queries about the history of the
churches.

Then there was all the business of trying to bring renewal
to two churches that had not experienced a great deal of the
gifts of the Holy Spirit. It wasn't easy being pulled almost
equally between two churches and trying to get some pattern of
worship, firstly that enabled experimentation with newer forms
of services and secondly that wasn't exhausting, especially at
Christmas! I realise that many clergy in the countryside have far
more than two parishes, but in a way the two-church dynamic
can be harder. I had to live in one of the parishes, and I know
that some in the other parish found this difficult. Although in
name I was Rector of a joint benefice, to many in either parish I
was always *their* Rector. Memories of what things have been like
in the old days can die hard.

Full-time church leadership can be a lonely occupation at
times, wherever you find yourself. We had moved to a strange
part of the country and a very different kind of situation to the
one we had been used to in the suburbs. I'll never forget standing in our rather large garden not long after moving. I had lit a
bonfire after a tiring afternoon of gardening and found myself
staring out across the field next to our house. It was a lovely
view, but so different actually to be living somewhere like that,
miles from where we had lived most of our lives. My one
thought was, 'What on earth have we done, moving here?'

As it was, we settled in well as a family and it was to prove a
fulfilling time in Somerset. We had our third child while we were
there and made many friends. We ended up staying there over
eight years. There were many battles to be fought. We were committed to bringing renewal into any church situation we found
ourselves. We hoped to do so in Templecombe and Horsington,

believing firmly that normal Christianity involves seeing the power of the Holy Spirit at work and God's supernatural gifts poured out on his people. I often thought it showed the Lord's sense of humour that I should become a 'country rector' and there was no way that I could be anything like the traditional image of a rural parson. I think some people simply thought I was bringing 'city ways' to the countryside, but the fact is people need Jesus, his forgiveness and his power, wherever they live.

Battles

Undoubtedly, there *are* differences in the countryside to living and working in suburbia, and I had a lot to learn about how the church operated. This included a lot more overlap with the local community, for example. I very much wanted to respect the history too, and I remember looking in awe at the list of rectors in both churches going back to mediaeval times. One of the churches, St Mary's Abbas and Templecombe, was founded in the year 888 AD as a mission church of Shaftesbury Abbey. The Abbess there was Ethelgeda, a daughter of King Alfred the Great. Who was I to think that I could make a huge difference in the great scheme of things and in the context of such a history? Inevitably, there was some opposition to change.

It's amazing when you live in a village, even one of 1,800 people or so like Templecombe, how the place can feel like it's the centre of the world. Relatively small things can take on a huge significance, especially when everyone around seems to know what's going on. One of the battles we had was with the choir situation in Templecombe. It was only a small choir, but it became obvious that certain attitudes needed dealing with, especially after the young male organist threatened to resign if things weren't sorted out.

To cut a long story short, the choir had to be told that we didn't want them singing the Psalm at Evening Prayer any more. It was not being sung well, and a few in the congregation had been complaining. In reality, it was only a symptom of other, deeper issues to do with power and attitudes towards worship. When the choir refused to do what we asked, we had to say that either they came the next Sunday and didn't sing the Psalm, or they wouldn't be singing at all. This was put in a letter signed by me and the churchwardens. I have to say, it was an extremely difficult thing to do and it certainly wasn't cold-blooded on my part.

In next to no time, I found myself being phoned up by a reporter from one of the local papers. It didn't really matter what I said, because the headline had already been written I think: 'Anger as church choir is axed.' The story appeared in another local paper as well, with yet another article by a columnist supporting me. Whatever the truth of the situation and however we tried to communicate it, inevitably as Rector I took all the blame. Being a village, it was difficult to walk anywhere without wondering who knew about what was going on. In reality, I'm not sure that many people who didn't come to church really cared, but at the time Jane and I felt very beleaguered in spite of the tremendous support from other church members.

Before I left Birmingham the Bishop at the time, Mark Santer, visited our parish and ended up chatting to me about the rural ministry I was about to undertake. He himself had been brought up in a country vicarage and said, 'In a village, you have to live with your mistakes; they'll be behind you in the queue at the post office.' Well I'd like to think they weren't all mistakes, but it's certainly true that you 'live with' your decisions, in the sense that the Bishop meant, on a daily basis.

There were many other challenges and battles in Somerset. These included a staffing issue at one of the schools that had wider implications, issues over building reordering (including pews) and events to do with modern versions of the Knights Templar. In the Middle Ages the original Templars had their southwest England headquarters in what was to become known as Temple Combe. St Mary's was actually in the next village of Abbas Combe in those days and had nothing to do with the Templars. Partly because of the ambiguities surrounding the history of the Templars, and partly because I wasn't happy with the ethos behind some of the modern so-called 'orders' of Knights Templar, as well as local politics which were involved, I wasn't happy to allow St Mary's to be used for investiture-type services.

Yet another rather bizarre set of events that got me into the newspapers, even two of the nationals, was the discovery of the remains of several Saxon people while Wessex Water were laying a new pipeline. After extensive examination, these remains were to be reburied in St Mary's churchyard under Home Office regulations but somehow they were acquired by a third party in the hope of displaying them publicly. In the end, the bones were reclaimed by the archaeologists and handed over to me for private burial. We even had a rather nice head-stone made for them. As it happens, I think the series of events served to build bridges in the community. Nevertheless, it was all upheaval I could have done without.

Looking back, these events were not earth shattering, even though they seemed so important at the time. Many other church leaders have gone through worse experiences, often over issues such as music in church or the removal of pews. Some of my battles in Somerset seemed to be to do with things in the community, and if I'm honest it's often worse when there are problems within the church fellowship. I've had my share of those as well, but mostly I've managed to keep out of the newspapers except for happy things since those days!

The security of our calling

Since moving to Benfleet in Essex there have still been the inevitable stresses of leading a church community. Some have been different to Somerset, others similar. The important thing is to be prepared to do what is necessary if it's what the Lord wants. My testimony really is that had I not faced up to what was going on in my life emotionally in previous years I don't think I would have survived in full-time church leadership. I guess I may not have got as far as being in such leadership in the first place, but having said that I might have learned to paper over the cracks as time went by.

In my situation, leadership is a joint calling, and to have Jane alongside me has been such a blessing. Something I haven't touched on is how strong she had to be in those early days before and since our marriage. I know that I was incredibly difficult to live with and I've no doubt that there are many women who would have simply given up. I believe that Jane's commitment to me was quite sacrificial. It's a testimony both to the grace of God and to her love and forbearance that she remained with me and was eventually able to share with me in the calling to full-time church leadership.

Criticism is something that many leaders cope with badly. We'd all like to be popular, if we're honest. We all need a degree of affirmation. Somehow church leaders hear the negative comments much more loudly than the positive ones, even when the latter outnumber the former. I therefore believe that it's particularly important for leaders to be secure in their calling to whatever situation they find themselves placed in. It doesn't mean that we should become overbearing and push through what we feel the Lord is saying without listening to others and involving them in shared vision and leadership. But it does mean that we can say to those who would oppose us that we are called to be God-pleasers and not man-pleasers. We therefore shouldn't *need* the approval of other people.

I still could have been carrying around with me in recent years a poor self-image and an unfulfilled need to feel important, while just not seeing that tendency towards envy of others. Had that been so, the weight of trying to please others and hearing criticism (which is often second-hand, of course) would have been too much to bear. Conflict, which is an inevitable part of change and particularly in a situation of Holy Spirit renewal, would have been unbearable. Too often leaders avoid conflict because they're afraid of the damage that might be done, especially to themselves. When that's the case change simply doesn't happen and, I would argue, the Kingdom is not advanced. We're not looking for conflict (remember the alpha male syndrome!) but if we're in the Kingdom business it will come, both without and within the church: "From the days of John the Baptist until now, the kingdom of heaven has been forcefully advancing, and forceful men lay hold of it." ' (Matthew 11:12).

Ultimately, the Christian's real calling is to be a child of God and to stand secure and firm in the knowledge of that. It doesn't matter what gifts we have, nor what office we might hold in the church. I think it's rather unfortunate that the Parable of the Talents in Matthew 25:14–30 has given us our word 'talent', which means we tend to think of it in terms of using our gifts and abilities. Actually, a talent was a unit of money and not an ability. In Luke's version, it's a 'mina' and not a talent anyway.

It seems to me the parable is about making the most of your life with what God has given you in *every* sense; gifts possibly, but also the fruit of your character, your relationships, your readiness to do his will, your commitment, your faithfulness, and so on. Those are the things that will determine whether he says to us when we stand before him, 'Well done, good and faithful servant!' Are we prepared to stand securely in our identity as children of God even if he were to take away our gifts and 'our' ministry?

The greatest need

I've described my own insecurities in terms of needing to feel important. I suppose if we asked the question, 'What is a man or woman's greatest need?' many of us would say, 'Love'. We all need love, of course, from other human beings and above all from our heavenly Father. But how is love expressed? It's expressed both in serving *and* in paying attention to someone, making them the object of our main interest. It's like in a marriage where we both love our partner in our actions and in our romantic concentration upon them. The same is true in a parent-child relationship. In other words, love is two sides of a coin, the doing and the feeling. Both of them are necessary for the object of love to be fulfilled. And where there is no fulfilment, there is continuing frustration.

If it's true that many of us go through life with a 'not OK' view of ourselves, we need to be prepared to see how this pans out in our own lives and in the lives of others. Sometimes people behave in ways that can make us angry or frustrated. If we could only see what lies behind the way they act (as well as what's behind our reaction to them), we might be able to respond differently. I've mostly described how my 'not OK-ness' resulted partly in jealous feelings. In fact, there are all sorts of things that can come out of people's poor view of themselves; a lack of self-worth leading to the inability to receive love from others (including a heavenly Father), issues of self-confidence and shyness, anxieties, phobias, perfectionism, drivenness, and so on.

All of these can lead to a degree of depression. Depression is obviously something that can have a physical cause, but so often it is only a symptom of other things. No amount of pills will deal with those causes. What's needed for most people, including those in the Christian community and in church leadership, is a degree of self-awareness and honesty. We need to acknowledge where we have problems and understand when we're playing emotional games. It takes courage, because not everyone likes to admit their weaknesses.

Note

1. This comes from an article in *The Times* reviewing Kate Ludeman and Eddie Erlandson, *Alpha Male Syndrome*, (Harvard Business School Press, 2006).

CHAPTER ELEVEN

THE ABSENT FATHER

The need for a child to learn appropriate behaviour in the human community is best met from its earliest years by good parents . . . male and female.

God is pure goodness. His will is always what is right. While we can make choices that are outside God's intention, these choices are certainly not rights. We have no rights to be other than God intends. So the issue is: 'does God intend children to be brought up without a father model?' If not, it is not a woman's right to have a baby on her own.[1]

Grumpy old man

I mentioned earlier that my family often accuse me these days of being a grumpy old man. As it happens, I am at that age where there seem to be many things around me that make me cross. I find myself agreeing with comments from all the other grumpy old men about a range of things from litter in the streets and dangerous driving to the loudness of fireworks and the commercialisation of Christmas. I suppose the problem with middle age is that you're old enough to have seen a lot of changes in society, but you're still young enough to think that getting angry about them can change things back. May the Lord protect me from my grumpiness!

The trouble is, when it comes to spiritual things as well I can find myself getting worked up. That's probably because there really have been an enormous number of changes in the spiritual state of society in recent years. I'd like to think my impatience here is maybe a little bit more godly. Not everything has been bad, and one must point to a lot of enlightened attitudes towards race, gender, disablement and so on that didn't exist before. People have greater opportunities, and prejudices in terms of class or otherwise have been highlighted, with many rights instigated that weren't there previously. However, there are also a lot of things that someone like me would class as disturbing. I wouldn't claim that this ever used to be a 'Christian' country, but there's no doubt that many things to do with Christianity have held our society together over many generations and we have seen the gradual erosion of these without convincing replacements.

One of these has to be the way family life has existed for so long in many quarters of society. I'm not naïve enough to suggest that things have always been rosy, and where oppression has existed within families I'm sure it's right that we should make it easier for people to seek help and to have their rights as individuals recognised. Nevertheless, statistics are proving that changes in patterns of family life are creating some worrying trends, particularly when it comes to children being brought up without both a father and a mother. UK Government figures show that the proportion of lone-parent families in the country is likely to become thirty-three per cent by 2010. Most lone-parent families are lone mothers. Only three per cent are lone fathers, and two per cent are widows or widowers.

In September 2006 The Children's Society launched 'The Good Childhood Enquiry' in order to find out just how deep changes go and what effect they have on people. Its launch report was able to set the scene dramatically and I think is worth quoting from:

> Childhood has changed significantly from that experienced by previous generations. New technology runs apace, while demographic changes mean that society today is increasingly diverse.

Family structures are changing. Between 1972 and 2004 the proportion of children in the UK living in single parent families more than tripled to twenty-four per cent (Summerfield and Gill, 2005). The UK leads Europe for the proportion of young people living in single parent or step families (Currie et al, 2004).

Research shows that changes in family structure, and the major events that these indicate, are an important factor in the well-being of children (Bradshaw et al, *op cit*). Our recent study of young runaways, for example, reveals that children living with one birth parent are twice as likely to have run away and children in step families are three times as likely to have run away as those living with both parents (Rees and Lee, 2005). What can we do to support the family, and the children and young people at the centre of this important unit, when it breaks down?[2]

Bringing it home

Politicians, educationalists, the news media and many others are asking all sorts of questions about the role of the family. What indeed can be done to 'support the family'? What are the effects that changes are having on young people? Statistics alone aren't enough to bring all this home to us. We have to realise that we are all affected in some way. The head teacher of a local primary school was telling me how one of her teachers asked her class to write about what they had done for the weekend. Half the children wrote about how they had spent the time away from their mothers with their 'real' fathers. When I asked how children at the school seem to deal with this emotionally, the answer was simply, 'Some cope, others don't.' Our town is not in a particularly difficult part of the world in terms of social deprivation, probably just reflecting the national trend.

When my parents split up it was very much against the norm. You didn't talk about things like that because there was still a degree of shame attached to the whole word 'divorce'. We have now seen an enormous increase in the divorce rate and in the number of people who live together and have children without getting married but still split up. 'Serial monogamy' seems to have become the trend for many, with children experiencing living with more than one stepfather during their lifetime.

Whatever we might think about this, the experts are telling us that such changes are definitely having an effect on the behaviour of children. We have already heard about the number of runaways from single-parent and 'step family' homes. We hear too how children from broken homes have problems with authority, often leading to dropping out of education and/or leading to crime. We hear about drug taking and alcoholism. We hear about the difficulties of forming relationships, especially with the opposite sex. We hear about how patterns of family break-up can continue through the generations, with those from broken homes unable to maintain commitment.

I asked my local head teacher about some of the changes in patterns of behaviour she had noticed in recent times. She thought the boys in particular are much more aggressive in the playground than they used to be. She wondered if it was something to do with the way fathers and sons interact, especially when engaging in horseplay (something that has always been a feature of many father-son relationships). It's OK to show your strength as a man, but it's equally acceptable to allow your son to win sometimes. That's how he learns to stand alone. If the father is unable to do this it might be because he feels the need to maintain power over the child, perhaps because he himself hasn't learned to be secure as a man. The son, who might feel inferior as a result, then retests this scenario in the playground as he seeks to dominate others.

If this is the case, could it be because so many children nowadays only see their fathers at weekends, in a rather false 'concentrated' situation? Is it because the fathers themselves have not learned helpful patterns in their own growing up? Of course, it's not just the boys that have problems. Girls are having to come to terms with the changes in society. But as my head teacher bore witness, girls generally show their needs much more outwardly. They are more likely to become eventually the primary carers in a family, so neediness and emotional intensity are worked out in their relationships, often with their mothers. Boys, on the other hand, have not had that intensity of emotional expression with their fathers and often tend to hide their feelings as a result.

I spoke to the director of a local counselling service about male-female trends and differences. It was encouraging to learn that more men were coming forward for counselling (sixty per cent female, forty per cent male as opposed to seventy to thirty per cent previously). However, men still find it incredibly difficult to know *how* to talk about their feelings, even if they know they are feeling something acutely. He thought that many men were exhibiting more anger these days. Abuse in the family, feelings of not being loved or of being rejected and so on are leading to misplaced aggression in all kinds of situations. When men have had problems relating to their father they often have difficulty relating to any kind of parent figure. I've mentioned problems I've had in the past relating to older men, often irrationally feeling inferior to them. For some, the authority thing can lead to misplaced anger as well.

Guilt

One wonders how much guilt there is around these days, despite the fact that divorce and family break-up is much more 'acceptable'. In an area such as where I live, many parents seem to want the school to provide excellent discipline, but if there's any suggestion that their child might be to blame in any way the response is often one of anger and indignation. Of course that could show general attitudes towards authority, but there might also be a sense of guilt hidden away about how they have brought up their own children.

I'm aware from witnessing how things affected my mother and from pastoral situations I've been embroiled with how complicated separation and divorce can be. I have already spoken about how I think divorce very often can be worse than death. Of course, to lose a spouse through death is a terrible thing and none of us would wish it on anyone, least alone ourselves. But at least there can be memories of happy times and indeed a happy marriage.

I know I'm generalising and sometimes a spouse's dying *can* lead to all sorts of difficult feelings in the one left behind. There might be guilt or similar emotions, especially if the marriage wasn't actually so happy. However, with divorce there's a much greater chance of things getting twisted. Love often turns to hatred and bitterness, leaving wounds that are difficult to heal. Also, there can be enormous feelings of guilt that perhaps you didn't do things right, or maybe you feel a failure as a husband/wife/human being.

My intention is not to make anyone who has been through this situation feel any more guilty than they do. I'm simply trying to point out that we are reaping what we sow as a society. Nor am I trying to argue the case against divorce as such. When I was young I felt very strongly that divorce was wrong per se. My only understanding of it then was where one party had been injured by the adultery of the other. My experience with the hurt that my parents' divorce had caused me personally meant I found it very hard to think of justifying circumstances. That's a fairly obvious reaction, I suppose. As time went by I could see quite clearly that my mother would be justified in remarrying. After all, it was not her fault that her husband had had an affair; at least that's how I saw it. The last thing I wanted was for her to be alone for the rest of her life, although sadly that's the way it was to be.

As a Christian later on, I needed to understand the whole question of divorce more broadly. My understanding was that in an ideal world divorce should not and need not happen. God himself knows what pain it can lead to; that's why he said, 'I hate divorce' (Malachi 2:16). Of course it's not his will that any couple should get divorced. However, Jesus does mention that marital unfaithfulness could be grounds for divorce (Matthew 5:31), and I was happy to believe that someone like my mother could get married again with a clear conscience. That would be the only grounds for considering divorce. However, over the years I have come to understand much more about how total breakdown in communication and, particularly, abuse might be considered grounds.

It's a huge subject, and one that has been dealt with in much more detail by theologians and church leaders than I can possibly cover here. Suffice to say, I would never tell someone being abused in a relationship that they should stay with their partner come what may. Physical abuse is more obvious, but psychological abuse can be just as devastating. The problem is, many other reasons are given by couples wanting to split up and it usually isn't black and white. For church ministers it can be a minefield, which is why churches need to have very well thought out guidelines if they consider undertaking the remarriage of divorcees.

What about the children?

> The conversation's civilized, we calmly nod our heads,
> You're smiling as you always do, but your napkin is in shreds.
> You'd like to run away; ah, who'll be the first to say
> About the children?[3]

As someone who has suffered as a result of my parents splitting up, and as a Christian leader involved often in helping people in the whole area of marriage, I know I have to be realistic. I have no idea if the tide will ever turn again and marriage in our society will be a redeemed institution. However, it doesn't stop me wishing more people would understand the nature of commitment. It seems to me that many people drift into living together and even having children long before they are prepared to make a lifelong commitment to each other. I think there must be an awful lot of women living with a partner who long for the promise of a permanent relationship from them, made with some kind of public declaration. After all, whatever we say about equality it is the women who bear the children and are usually the primary carers. In a sense, they have the most to lose and need security. Figures I have already quoted show that ninety-seven per cent of lone-parent families in the UK involve lone mothers.

When it comes to marriage itself, it seems to me that it's far too easy for people simply to walk away rather than working at things. If only they would 'give it a proper go', perhaps if necessary going to see a marriage guidance counsellor who can help them be honest in their communication. Of course there is a big question: if a marriage involves a huge amount of unpleasant conflict, is it better for the children that the parents split up or that they stay together? Also, what I've said about the unpleasantness of divorce, recrimination and so on isn't always the case. I've heard of plenty of couples who simply didn't get on well when they were married, but can remain good friends while apart. Everyone says they are happy with the arrangement, and will always tell you the children are as well. But can they be sure of this?

Again, if the situation involves violence or extreme verbal conflict, and the one partner isn't prepared to give any ground and seek help with the other, then the protection of the children at least must be a consideration. However, I know from my own experience and from talking to other people over the years that a child ultimately wants one thing – *for their mum and dad to be together*. My plea would be for people to give much more serious consideration to the effect that their splitting up will have on their children and at least to try to find ways of healing their marriage or relationship.

I've often heard people say that they've tried everything (to get their partner to listen, to communicate their needs, etc), but it's not always the case. If someone really won't budge on the issue of going to see a third party such as a counsellor then, yes, there are problems. But so many don't ever reach that stage, rather people seek escape from what they see as pain. If only people had decent marriage preparation as well, thinking long and hard about what they are really entering into ('till death us do part'). Unfortunately, love really can be blind and many people when they're in love, with all the associated strong feelings, find it impossible to step back and be realistic about themselves and their partner.

Mother and father together

Why is it so important that a child has their mother and father together? For one thing, we have been created male and female, but we have to learn maleness and femaleness within the context of a family. Role models are important. When we're young, we actually learn about sexuality not from personal development classes at school but from how things work out with our parents. I mentioned before about the possibility of homosexuality developing if a child fails to make a proper psychological separation from one parent and a proper bonding to the other:

> He needs two forces to break that primary tie (to the mother). *One*, he needs his mother to help him cope with moving away from her, because there's an emotional umbilical cord joining them, and if the mother won't let go of her end, it'll be very difficult for him to get free. And *two*, he needs his father to love him and want him as a fellow male.[4]

This is not a popular view in the current climate, and some homosexual activists will not consider the possibility of a psychological 'cause' and therefore the option of a 'cure'.

But the issue is much wider than homosexuality. Personally, I was never aware of that on my horizon anyway. Perhaps my father's male role model had been sufficient in earlier years, or perhaps my uncle had been an important factor. The broader picture is how we develop as men and women in our sexuality and in our confidence as people. Without wishing to return to an age when women were downtrodden and only the men ever did the 'important' stuff, I nevertheless want to argue along with John Eldredge that women need to learn how to be women and men need to learn how to be men:

> My mother would often call me 'sweetheart,' but my father called me 'tiger.' Which direction do you think a boy would want to head? He will still turn to his mother for comfort (who does he run to when he skins his knee?), but he turns to Dad for adventure, for the chance to test his strength, and most of all, to get the answer to his question.[5]

This is not being chauvinistic, simply recognising that God has made men and women different, with equally important but complementary roles in life. I believe contraception has freed women enormously in terms of being able to choose when to have children, to seek careers, and so on. I wouldn't want to turn the clock back, although I'm sure we need to be careful. For example, some women are leaving having children until it is biologically much more dangerous or even too late.

The whole thing about equality is that men need to learn it too. They have a vital role in bringing up children as well as women. Even just being a role model isn't enough. Look at what Robin Skynner has to say:

> It's very interesting that the evidence in fact suggests that fathers can't *make* their sons masculine simply by setting a very masculine model themselves. Nor by just putting pressure on them to behave in that way, either. In fact this can have the opposite effect! It's where the fathers are masculine *and also loving*, supportive, and engage sometimes in the day-to-day care of their children that they produce sons and daughters both sexually confident.[6]

When we hear that, I think some of us might find ourselves saying, 'Where have all the fathers gone?' There is a responsibility here that I'm afraid many men don't understand.

Equally, let me say that I know there are many men who long

to be able to fulfil their role but cannot. The problem is, when a relationship has broken up a woman will often be all too aware of the need for a male role model for their child or children. She will of course probably seek to find the right person to fulfil that, but it often means that the child's natural father can be pushed out of the picture. Fathers' groups in the UK point out that forty per cent of divorced fathers lose contact with their children after two years. The same percentage of mothers admits to 'thwarting contact' between children and their fathers.

We can't generalise, of course, and many stepfathers no doubt fulfil their roles admirably. However, nothing can fully make up for the emotional trauma a child goes through when Dad is no longer around. My brother and I stopped seeing our father because we couldn't cope with re-living the separation every time we returned home to Mum. I'll never know how I would have reacted to a stepfather. As I said, I certainly wanted my mother to be happy and would have wanted her to remarry. I suppose for most women this would be the logical course to pursue. The sad thing in our society is that many women are ending up having a succession of boyfriends, none of whom can replace the real father. Have those women, and those men for that matter, managed to learn from the past or do they simply take the same problems into each relationship?

Nor can we underestimate the value of our parents just being there. It's all very well for children to go and spend a day or a weekend with their father, but it can never be the same to have a 'treat dad' as simply having him around. It only gets more complicated as children get older anyway. My experience of having teenagers is that they don't want to be doing stuff with their parents all the time; in fact often you can be more of an embarrassment to them in public if truth be known. What they do want is for you to be there for them when need arises. This includes the need to talk at the most surprising times of day or night!

Effects

What are the long-term effects in all this? Well of course, I can only speak from personal experience about how an absent father has affected me. For some people the absentee is the mother, although as we've heard this tends to be a small percentage. Nor can I speak with any personal authority about the effects of an absent father upon a daughter. Obviously, for a girl there won't be the same issues of lacking a masculine role model if the father isn't around, but some of the emotional damage is bound to be the same even if it's true that women can deal with their feelings better.

Let me say something else here. When we speak about an 'absent' parent, we might not be talking necessarily about a physical absence. Absent can also mean literally 'inattentive, abstracted in mind' (*Concise Oxford Dictionary*). I spoke earlier about the basic need in all of us for attention, something we look to get primarily from our parents in the early years. That attention might be lacking for all sorts of reasons. We might have lacked a mother's attention because of her own emotional agenda. Where a mother's needs are great and she is unable to give as she should all sorts of problems can be caused for a child. This is not to mention what happens when a mother's need means she can't let go. I know we will always be seen as children by our mothers to an extent, but as with most things it's a matter of degree. The emotional umbilical cord is never severed in some families, which can lead to all kinds of problems for the children later in life, not least in their marriages.

Alternatively of course we may have lacked a father's attention. I've heard many people speak about how their fathers were emotionally distant, unable to express love or affirmation, unable perhaps to deal adequately with conflict. These fathers may have lived in the family home but they still left a great emotional hole in their children's lives. We can think of all sorts of reasons for this pattern of behaviour. Generations past have encouraged fathers to be distant to an extent, upholding the stiff upper lip approach to work, family and life in general. We shouldn't really blame anyone for this and often hard working environments and long hours out of the house didn't exactly give fathers a head start. Not only that, but let's remember what we considered earlier about the effects of war and other social traumas and conditions.

I can only describe the effects on me, as I've tried to do in this book. I haven't ever run away from home. I haven't turned to crime, nor to alcohol or drugs. I haven't dropped out of the education system. To a large extent I have coped with authority; when you think that I was a Welsh nationalist and a bit of a republican, it's really quite something that I should have ended up swearing allegiance to the Queen as a 'Clerk in Holy Orders' in the Church of England! However, as you've read there have been many internal conflicts I've had to try to come to terms with. When I look back, things could have been very different. I could have easily rebelled much more overtly. Were it not for a strong and supportive mother and her family, I may well have felt like running away from home early on. Later, I could have started taking drugs or drinking heavily. When things were really difficult I could have tried to numb the pain with these things. My marriage could easily have failed miserably; as it is, I'm so grateful for a patient and understanding wife.

What has been the difference for me? Undoubtedly I can be thankful for a degree of middle-class stability in terms of education and so on. I can be thankful for that extended family on my mother's side. As many of the conflicts within me were in a sense bottled up or avoided until my early twenties, when they were almost forced to the surface, I have to point to the fact that I had become a Christian. My relationship with the Lord Jesus Christ was the key factor in bringing inner healing. However, as I've tried to say all along it's been so important to try to step outside myself and identify feelings and conflicts in order to bring them to the Lord for healing.

Self-confidence

I've mentioned lack of self-confidence. This is an issue for many people, but so few seem to progress in this area. I need to make something clear here. Some Christians will say that it's wrong to use the phrase *self*-confidence. After all, aren't we meant to rely totally on God? It is certainly true that the Apostle Paul makes much of our need to rely on God's strength and not our own: 'For when I am weak, then I am strong.' (2 Corinthians 12:10). There have been many times in my life when I've been out of my depth and called on the Lord for his help. In many areas we do need to acknowledge our insufficiencies; decisions and choices we have to make, relationships, witnessing to non-believers, and many more. Most church leaders I've come across will tell you how much they rely on his strength in plenty of situations where people assume they're completely confident.

Having said that, it's easy to over spiritualise the whole thing. I believe that God is interested in every aspect of our lives, but he still leaves us to deal with everyday things with a certain amount of common sense and self-sufficiency. For example, we should be able to converse reasonably freely with *most* people without having to cry out to him in prayer every time. We ought to be able to smile at people in the street without worrying if they don't smile back. We ought to be able to get on a bus, order a train ticket, decide what to buy in a shop (within reason economically), and make a variety of smaller decisions with the normal human resources he has given us. When any of these things become difficult the issue is not about a lack of confidence in God, rather a lack of self-confidence. I still need God's help in many areas of my life where I might lack confidence, but the whole thing about getting through everyday life is to do with a general healing and setting free of the personality.

The same is true for that related condition, shyness. How is it that I can stand up in front of people and preach, indeed enjoy the experience, when once I was almost too shy to answer the front door? I want to deal with this more fully in the final chapter, but for now let me say what I think shyness really is. It's actually a form of self-centredness. Hear me right please; I am not saying 'selfishness'. But in the end shyness is really saying that I'm the centre of the universe, which is why everybody must be looking at me. I don't like having my picture taken or having attention brought to me because I'm concerned they won't think much of me. The fact is, most people probably won't care and for all you know they might be thinking the same way about themselves.

Shyness, self-consciousness, whatever you want to call it, in a sense is seeing everything from your own perspective and only yours. Are people really looking at you? Of course, deep down it may well be to do with a poor self-image. Maybe it's because in your own eyes you're simply 'not OK' for reasons described earlier. The question is, are you prepared simply to live with it? Self-awareness is the beginning of dealing with self-consciousness. Sometimes in a public place I've suddenly realised that subconsciously I've been thinking people are noticing me. Maybe the CCTV is focused exclusively on me. That's a bit of silly paranoia of course, but I sometimes wonder how many others are subconsciously thinking the same thing at the same time! At least I've caught myself doing it and can adjust my mindset accordingly. Such self-consciousness can extend to many areas of life, from worrying about our noisy children in church to being amongst the 1 in 14 men who don't like using public conveniences (an astounding statistic I heard on the radio). Mind you, Britain does have more CCTV cameras than most countries in the world, a fact which won't help people with problems of self-consciousness!

Then there's perfectionism. Many people confess to having problems with this. I have always wanted things to be just right, especially when making something or doing a job like decorating. Sometimes this trait can be very annoying and time-consuming. One day, I realised that it was because I needed approval from people, and only the perfect would do. But who was it I was really trying to please? Whose approval did I seek? As I thought about it, I realised that it was actually my absent father. It must have gone right back to the time when I perhaps blamed myself for his going, or maybe even beyond that. Perhaps he was never good at giving praise and affirmation; I've heard plenty of others speak about their parents and their own perfectionism in this way. Certainly, I would have given anything to have my father back. The reali-sation of what lay behind my perfectionism began a process of setting me free from it.

Tied in with all this can be a sense of having to prove some-thing all the time. I know I've had that problem before now and I can't help feeling a lot of people do as well, including quite a few church leaders I've met over the years. If there were any-one we really needed to please, it would be the Lord rather than other people. Since our forgiven status, along with our strengths and abilities, come from him anyway there is nothing we can prove to him.

The very present Father

Perhaps one of the most written about subjects in Christian circles in recent years has been about rediscovering the father-hood of God. It is true that many people have difficulties in their relationship with God in terms of accepting his love as a father who would do no harm, indeed who loves to give good gifts to his children *because* they are his children (Matthew 7:11). We cannot earn his love. The Holy Spirit is someone who wants to bring us into a full and deeper relationship with our heav-enly Father. That means a relationship at every level, including our emotions.

It's obvious really, isn't it? How can we have a truly emo-tional relationship with him as our heavenly Father if our view of a father, subconscious or not, has been tainted in some way. For me, it's been partly a question of realising that I'm usually not to blame if bad things happen in life. I found myself thinking subconsciously that such things as having a flat tyre on the car were a kind of punishment. Then I came to realise it's not because 'the world', or even God, had somehow got it in for me. I'm not a bad person, at least no worse than anyone else. I may be a sinner, but he's forgiven me and simply wants to put his arms around me. Nor will he ever abandon me. These are not things that everybody will relate to, but having said that I do believe that similar kinds of thoughts and reactions are actually very common amongst both men and women.

Being renewed in the Holy Spirit is about receiving good gifts from our heavenly Father and allowing him to 'put his arms around you' and show you in your deepest being how in his eyes you're 'OK'. For me, if you like, it's been about the Holy Spirit teaching my soul that it wasn't my fault that my human father left, nor that I need to prove anything to my heavenly Father. That's because he loves me for who I am, and actually I'm important in his eyes:

> This is the heart of prayer: to learn to be loved by God and to give ourselves in joyful abandonment back to him. When Jesus says that we can call God 'Father', it is not a title with which to address him, but the gateway to a passionate love affair that will consume our hearts and energise the very core of our beings. It is the path to maturity.[7]

Do we feel guilty about enjoying the presence of God? So many of us see serving God as our main purpose in life, but actually that isn't true. Many of us have heard the first question and answer of the Westminster Shorter Catechism: 'What is the chief end of man? Man's chief end is to glorify God, and to enjoy him forever.' We might have heard it, but do we really believe it? I want to *enjoy* being in my Father's presence and if there's anything in this life that prevents that, I want to be free of it.

The wound

So there we are; just some of the effects of the absent father, and perhaps to a lesser extent the absent mother. Whether they are absent physically or absent emotionally isn't the real issue – it's to what degree we are affected that is important. Society needs to understand what changes are taking place with family life. It may not be possible to turn the clock back, but I do believe that we need to see more support for family life and marriage as it was meant to be. This includes financial benefits, but more importantly to underline commitment as something we need to rediscover. Simplistic it may be, but I know that as a child I just wanted my mum and dad to stay together. My father's going was like a bereavement, perhaps worse. I know that because not long after he'd gone my mother found me copying out some words from the deaths page of a newspaper. They seemed to sum up how I felt, but it's probably as well she persuaded me not to send them to my dad as I had planned.

So long as we live in a fallen world, there will be imperfection in every area of life, not least the family. How things will pan out in terms of social problems and individuals having emotional difficulties, we can only guess. Already, we know that more and more people are suffering in ways that medicine can't help. John Eldredge, concerned particularly for the effects upon men, speaks of the 'wound':

> Every man carries a wound. I have never met a man without one. No matter how good your life may have seemed to you, you live in a broken world full of broken people. Your mother and father, no matter how wonderful, couldn't have been perfect. She is a daughter of Eve, and he a son of Adam. So there is no crossing through this country without taking a wound.[8]

I believe that the Christian community has much to offer in terms of rebuilding people's lives and pointing them to the only one who can heal the wound fully; a wound that is so often the result of the 'absent parent' scenario. The coming days will certainly be a challenge for us all.

Notes

1. Bishop Graham Dow, 'Are Fathers Necessary?', *Carlisle Diocesan News*, October 2006.
2. 'The Good Childhood Enquiry Launch Report', (The Children's Society, 18th September 2006).
3. Tom Paxton, *About the Children*, (United Artists Music Ltd).
4. Robin Skynner and John Cleese, *Families and How to Survive Them*, (Methuen, 1983, p. 247).
5. John Eldredge, *Wild at Heart*, (Nelson, 2001, p. 64).
6. Skynner and Cleese, *op. cit.* pp. 245–246.
7. Stuart Lees, *Transforming Life*, (Kingsway Publications, 1997, p. 213).
8. Eldredge, *op. cit.* p. 72.

CHAPTER TWELVE

SELF-CENTRED OR GOD-CENTRED?

Looking within

> This is the way we are with our wound, especially men. We bury it
> deep and never take it out again. But take it out we must, or better,
> enter into it.[1]

I've spent much of this book thinking about how important it is
for us all to be able to look within ourselves and try to grasp at
least a little of what makes us tick as human beings. I reminded
us how complicated we are and what wonderful creatures we are
in terms of the work of God. My plea is for all of us to step back
sometimes and think about what lies behind the way we react to
other people and the emotions we feel which we don't always
understand. Of course, it's not an easy thing to do, especially if
we recognise that we are hurting to a certain degree. A lot of
people would prefer to ignore any self-examination, perhaps
because they're afraid of what they might find, or perhaps
because they simply have no time in the busyness of life.

I've tried to include some of the things I've learned over the
years, knowing that I couldn't make this a textbook even if I
wanted to. Not being a professional psychologist I'd probably
describe myself more as an observer of human nature, as well
as someone who tries to help others in their journey of faith and
wholeness of being. I think the best way of sharing ideas is to

tell one's own story, and that's what I've tried to do without being too introspective. Everyone's story is different and it might be that you relate only to some of what I've been saying, or maybe to none at all. Nevertheless, we all need to recognise the imperfections of this fallen world and how much we need healing and restoring by the Holy Spirit of our risen Lord.

Some Christians proclaim what we might call a triumphalist Gospel. They declare that at conversion we appropriate all we need, not only for forgiveness of sins but also for the instant healing of all our pains. We simply shouldn't be suffering depression, fears or anxieties any longer. I wouldn't deny for a minute that when I began to follow Christ I became a new creation (2 Corinthians 5:17). I entered into a new relationship with my Creator and indeed received all his promises as a child of God. I do believe that the Christian life involves much in the sense of standing on those promises, sometimes with an act of the will. For example, I can choose to believe that God is stronger than the devil because the Bible says so (1 John 4:4) and I can decide to use the authority I have in Jesus' name over all sorts of things.

But even triumphalism cannot deny that conversion is only the beginning of a journey of faith. This journey involves our 'sanctification'; that is, becoming like Jesus in terms of turning from sin and developing character. This is something that takes a lifetime. Paul reminds us that we are not perfect; we see 'but a poor reflection as in a mirror' (1 Corinthians 13:12). Meanwhile, we should indeed look within to evaluate how we are doing:

Let us examine our ways and test them, and let us return to the LORD. (Lamentations 3:40)

Examine yourselves to see whether you are in the faith; test yourselves. (2 Corinthians 13:5)

My argument is simply that examining and testing your ways are not only about looking at your sins; they are also about looking at what lies behind those sins. If anger is your problem, why are you getting angry? If you're prone to gossip, what is it that makes you feel the need to do so? Of course, ultimately sin is rebellion against God, and as such is mostly wilful. That's why we're called not to gratify the desires of our sinful nature but to keep in step with the Spirit and allow good fruit to be produced in us (Galatians 5:16–26). It often *is* about an act of the will, about choosing to go a certain way. However, while keeping all that constantly in mind we might still need to go deeper in order to understand the origins of our difficulties with doing it God's way. I've given the example of jealousy in my own life. I will readily concede that jealousy is a sin, but I've only been able to stop myself firstly when I've actually managed to recognise it, secondly when I've understood something of the causes of it, and thirdly when I've been able to ask for healing from those causes.

Turning it around

So what is the process by which healing will come in the context of renewal in the Holy Spirit? I've made much of self-awareness, allowing feelings to be exposed so that they can be dealt with by our adult mind. Certainly, the person-centred therapy I experienced originally was very much based on this. However, on its own I'm not convinced it was enough. I would argue strongly that I had to work in cooperation with the Holy Spirit so that he could do his work in me. Yes, I could 'deal' with feelings much better by understanding them, but the Spirit still had to bring healing at my request. As I brought these things to the Lord Jesus and prayed for his hand to reach out to me, so I submitted to his own brand of 'therapy'.

As I've said all along, I don't believe there is anything wrong with taking the best of what the world has to offer, including from the whole area of psychology. In terms of physical illness Christians don't reject the use of medicines, although it's not a bad thing to question the overuse of drugs, particularly perhaps when it comes to dealing with things like depression. The coun-selling centre director I was talking to mentioned what I think most of us might know, that people often go for help suffering from depression but frequently the cause of it is a phobia, an anxiety, or something similar. When I first sought help I may have been exhibiting depression outwardly, but it was not actually the illness. True depression can have many causes and does need to be dealt with professionally in most cases.

However, as a Christian I do want to be discerning about what's on offer. Personally, I'm very wary of anything that involves opening the mind up to external influences. That's why I'm wary of hypnotism and certain 'new' therapies that actually owe much to ancient eastern practices, often involving meditative techniques that refer to spiritual powers. As far as I'm concerned, any external spiritual influence that is not attributed to the Lord Jesus Christ is off-limits. Call that narrow if you like, but I'm too aware of the nature of good and evil in this world. Ultimately, only God is good and spiritual things that are not of him can be neither good in the true sense of the word nor neutral.

Person-centred therapy, helpful though it is, only goes so far. As well as that, there is a clue in its very name that limits it. It's not intrinsically bad to be 'person-centred' if it means looking within to find answers, but there comes a point when we need to become centred elsewhere. I want to argue that no one will be fully whole psychologically by continually looking into themselves. Healing is in fact a balance between looking within and looking beyond ourselves to Jesus and to his Kingdom. It is in fact about becoming 'God-centred', and indeed 'other-people-centred', instead of self-centred.

What do I mean by that? Basically, it's to do with what fills your mind and occupies your attention. I'll give a simple example. I don't wish in any way to deny the validity of singleness; many people have to live on their own, or indeed choose to do so. However, I know how living in a busy family occupies you with the needs of others. The demands of family life involve being concerned for others, very often when you don't feel like it. Children have needs, as does your spouse, and at times you might feel that you have 'lost' your self in them. You certainly need your space sometimes, but the sheer energy you pour into the family dynamic means you have less time to dwell on your own needs.

To put it in an old-fashioned way, you make sacrifices. Of course, you don't mind doing it because you love your family. I suppose it's ironic that my original difficulties came about from being involved emotionally with another human being, but that's just how God ended up dealing with me. I'm pretty sure that if you have a busy family like mine you'll know what I mean when I talk about how your needs are somehow sub-sumed into the family as a whole. Of course you might worry about your family, but your own needs are set in a much larger context.

Let's project that same principle onto our relationship with God. I have spoken about the need to feel important that I think is in most, if not all, human beings. However, that feeling of importance, that 'new shoes glow', will only be a lasting one if it comes from basking in the presence of our heavenly Father. What that means is that we can only find true worth in relation to him and therefore to a greater framework. Your ultimate pleasure comes from giving him pleasure, by being the obedi-ent child he smiles upon.

You can't please him by trying to be better in your own strength, but you can please him by being open to his Spirit, with all that might mean in his working in and through you. And if you put your energy, your heart, mind, soul and strength, into seeking him you will find eventually that you have been rescued from self-centredness. Listen to what Jesus says:' "Whoever finds his life will lose it, and whoever loses his life for my sake will find it." ' (Matthew 10:39).

Ostensibly, he was talking about eternal salvation; 'don't hang on to this life as if it's all there is, and you'll gain eternal life.' However, salvation isn't just about booking your ticket to heaven, it's about being made whole in this life as well. Therefore, losing yourself in him means truly finding yourself.

True gratification

In talking about gaining self-confidence and importance (in what I believe is the right sense of the word), I've generally tried to avoid using the word 'self-esteem'. This is a popular word in psychology and one that has been used by Christians as well on occasions. The problem with it lies in its literal meaning; 'Confidence in one's own worth or abilities' (*Compact Oxford Dictionary*). Yes, I want to know that I do have worth and I do have abilities. I can be confident because of that, but actually my worth only comes from my status in relation to God. Therefore, the ultimate goal of inner healing and renewal is not my own esteem or gratification within themselves, but my gratification in him. John Piper puts it like this:

> [Ask yourself:] 'Do you feel most loved by God because He makes much of you, or because He frees you to enjoy making much of Him for ever?' This is the test of whether our craving for the love of God is a craving for the blood-bought, Spirit-wrought capacity to see and glorify God by enjoying Him forever, or whether it is a craving for Him to make us the centre and give us the pleasures of esteeming ourselves. Who, in the end, is the all-satisfying Treasure that we are given by the love of God: self or God?[2]

In other words, his ultimate goal in setting me free is that I might be free to love him. That's actually what he made me for in the first place. If we take this further, we will find that we want to serve him because to do so is a pleasure. Then, we will find ourselves becoming lost in him in the way I've tried to describe above. Oh, that I could serve him wholeheartedly in a way that 'pours me out' (2 Timothy 4:6). When you read about the heroes of the faith in the New Testament, throughout history and today, you hear about people who lose their lives (sometimes physically) but find themselves in the Lord. I read about Brother Yun in *The Heavenly Man*[3] with nothing but admiration and I find myself wondering about the state of

Christianity in the west. We have become so consumerist and self-centred in our faith.

Sadly, this kind of attitude is exposed in the way many of us behave in church life. We've become used to things being done for us by other people, including worship services, or we're not satisfied unless everything is done exactly how we want. How often have you heard someone say, 'I enjoyed the worship,' or 'I didn't enjoy the worship today, it didn't do anything for me'? Surely what matters is if God enjoys the worship! A consumerist spirituality considers what I can get out of church, not what I can give to it. Taken to the extreme, people become 'spiritual gypsies', hopping from church to church until they find exactly what they want. Of course, they never do find it.

To become God-centred literally 'takes you out of yourself'. And totally tied in with it is to become other-people-centred. People sometimes accuse Christians of living a blinkered existence. I think the opposite is true. If I am truly centred upon God and upon his purposes, if I really want to serve him and do his will, then I am bound to have a much greater awareness. This awareness is *firstly* of the needs of my brothers and sisters within the body of Christ and *secondly* of the needs of the world. Loving God goes with loving others. John Piper again: 'Is my own native and insatiable longing for happiness seeking its fulfilment by drinking deeply at the fountain of God's mercy, then letting it spill over in love into the life of my neighbour?'[4]

Do you see then how God dealt with my shyness? He began by showing me where it came from, a sense of lack of worth or 'not OK-ness'. He then wrapped his arms around me supernaturally as only the Holy Spirit can do, allowing me to feel important as his child. Next, he called me to be centred upon him and upon others. In doing all this, he made me realise that what he thinks about me is what matters, not what other people think. Because my mind is not always centred upon me, it knows that people are not always all 'looking at me' and evaluating me. Even if I'm standing up and preaching in front of them my confidence comes from what he thinks, not what they think. In practical terms it helped that I began singing and playing the guitar in front of people. I slowly turned from a quivering jelly into a more confident performer. However, that was only one context and I needed to overcome shyness in a lot of others too.

Why is God-centredness important?

This principle of being centred on God is so important because it affects every aspect of our lives. For one thing, we can move on and not be stuck in the same emotional place we might have been in for years. We can begin to look beyond our own needs to the needs of others. Yes, we need to experience healing for the past, but the time comes when we have to leave certain things where they belong – behind us:

> It is crucial to fix our eyes on Christ and not to go looking for the problems and wounds of the past. We look first to Christ and invite the Holy Spirit to bring to the surface whatever emotions or attitudes are hidden beneath our consciousness. It is God's work to 'bubble up' these things, and not our job to find them. Only in this way will we be kept from introspection and an unhealthy obsession with our own needs and wants.[5]

God-centredness is the key to real victory over the devil. We looked at spiritual warfare and how Satan wants dominion over our minds. One of his best tricks is actually to keep us looking at ourselves. He might even make us think *too much* about the spiritual warfare side of things so that he gets more attention than he deserves. Both guilt about sin and a tendency to lick our wounds, instead of letting God deal with them as we move on in our walk with him, can keep us locked in a permanent sort of depression. Dr Martyn Lloyd-Jones wrote about this:

> Turn now to another category – depression and discouragement. This is one of the most remarkable manifestations of the activity of

the devil. He does it with non-Christians as well as with Christians. He depresses the mind. He does it generally by making us concentrate overmuch on ourselves. He keeps us looking at ourselves and examining ourselves, always looking at the past, at something we did in the past which we should not have done. He will keep us looking back until we are utterly depressed.[6]

God-centredness is the only true way to fulfil our vocation, both to be children of God and to accomplish whatever he calls us to do in joining in his mission to the world. It will mean we are not burdened by having to get our kudos from other people. It will mean we don't have to compete with others in whatever ministry we are seeking to exercise. It is worth thinking about some examples of this in the Bible. There are two particular examples that strike me, as well as Jesus himself.

Moses was described as the 'man of God', who fulfilled one of the greatest acts in history as he led God's people out of slavery towards the Promised Land. But we know that Moses lacked self-confidence. He was shy and felt he couldn't speak in front of Pharaoh. It's true that the Lord gave him Aaron to speak on his behalf, but he still had to do an awful lot in Egypt and beyond. When there were constant challenges to his authority from his own people, rather than reacting by trying to defend his authority he always did the only thing he knew; he turned to the Lord. I believe he was not only seeking what to do but was reaffirming his security, which came through his close relationship with his heavenly Father. Exodus 33:11 tells us that 'the LORD would speak to Moses face to face, as a man speaks with his friend. Then Moses would return to the camp . . .' Moses was not just the man of God, he was the friend of God!

My other example comes from the New Testament. John the Baptist was a man with a successful ministry. People were flocking to him to hear what he had to say and to be baptised by him. Then, he had to stand aside to allow the 'main man' to take the glory. I think the way John the Evangelist puts it in his Gospel is very illuminating:

Now John also was baptising at Aenon near Salim, because there was plenty of water, and people were constantly coming to be baptised. (This was before John was put in prison.) An argument developed between some of John's disciples and a certain Jew over the matter of ceremonial washing. They came to John and said to him, 'Rabbi, that man who was with you on the other side of the Jordan – the one you testified about – well, he is baptising, and everyone is going to him.'

To this John replied, 'A man can receive only what is given him from heaven. You yourselves can testify that I said, "I am not the Christ but am sent ahead of him." The bride belongs to the bridegroom. The friend who attends the bridegroom waits and listens for him, and is full of joy when he hears the bridegroom's voice. That joy is mine, and it is now complete. He must become greater; I must become less.' (John 3:23–30)

I wonder how many of us would have reacted like John in that situation. Would we perhaps have felt threatened? It's easy for us to say that John was a special person with a special calling; it's easy to say that he was given prophetic utterance about his role as the one preparing the way for the Messiah. But ultimately John was still human. He had built up a following and had the ear of many important people. He could have gone far in human terms. He could easily have chosen to ignore his calling as the voice of one crying in the desert, 'Make straight the way for the Lord.' Instead, he very clearly created the environment which allowed Jesus to fulfil his role by declaring him as the one from heaven, the Lamb of God who would take away the sin of the world and bring eternal life to believers.

Not only that, but we know that John went on to speak out against what he saw as wrong or hypocritical, risking the wrath of Herod. We know that it was in fact to lead to his death. What made a man like that apparently not care about his own well-being and status? How could he say that he must become less? Surely, complete security in his relationship with God is the answer. That was the only antidote to seeking worldly glory.

His fulfilment, indeed one might say his *enjoyment*, came from knowing exactly who he was. Becoming 'less' didn't mean that he was going to become less of a person. The irony is that the exact opposite would be true; in letting Jesus take the glory, John would truly find himself and what we might even call greatness. Had he tried to find himself in a worldly sense, he would have lost his true identity.

I think there is a lesson for all of us in John the Baptist. To be able to rejoice in what God is doing in other people's lives is a great freedom, once you are secure with God. Even if others end up more 'successful' or gifted or maybe leading bigger churches, we can enjoy the whole thing because we're enjoying God. We're enjoying him for who he is and who we are, not because of any gifts or status we might have or wish we had.

The supreme example

'Your attitude should be the same as that of Christ Jesus', said Paul, as he spoke about how Jesus emptied himself of his divine status and became our servant (Philippians 2:5). So, yes, to an extent there is an act of our will needed in order to adopt that attitude. But my testimony is of how difficult that has been for me. I had to recognise in the first place that I couldn't serve others properly while I was burdened with an unfulfilled need to feel important. Only when I finally identified the problem, along with the jealousies that resulted, could I ask for healing.

And from whom was I asking healing? To so many people God is an abstract concept, or at best a rather distant creator. They might cry out to him for help at times in their lives, but it's all a bit of a lottery as to whether he'll hear them. How can he possibly understand how they feel? When I've spoken in such personal terms about the healing of the Holy Spirit I've done so because I know *he* is in fact personal. He is the very Spirit of the risen Jesus himself (Philippians 1:19, Galatians 4:6). Jesus walked this earth as one of us and went through the same experiences, including temptation. He does know what it's like for us (Hebrews 2:18 and 4:15). The Spirit he sends into our hearts is the only person qualified to deal with us at every level of our being.

But what about this whole servanthood thing? If Jesus was the Son of God, then surely it was easy for him to do anything, even to lay aside his own divinity? We need to remember that, yes, he was the Son of God, but he was also the Son of Man. The Word became flesh; he lived as a man, Jesus of Nazareth. When he per-formed miracles it was because the Holy Spirit had come upon him, and when he lived a sinless life it was because he resisted temptation. In theory, he could have worshipped at the devil's feet in order to rule over the world, but he didn't. He could have gloried in his status; instead, he chose to obey his Father and take the route of serving which eventually led to the cross.

In John 13 we see an amazing illustration he gave to his dis-ciples of what he was really all about when he washed their feet. He was the Master, the Christ, the Son of the living God, yet he performed the task of a lowly servant. No wonder Peter couldn't cope with it. How could Jesus do this? The key lies in verse 1:

Jesus knew that the time had come for him to leave this world and go to the Father. Having loved his own who were in the world, he now showed them the full extent of his love.

Jesus knew why he had come. He knew where he was going. Above all, he knew who he was. He was totally secure in his relationship with his Father. I want to suggest that it was only because of this security he had as the man Jesus of Nazareth that he could perform such a menial act. 'You call me "Teacher" and "Lord", and rightly so, for that is what I am," he says; yet he could also be their servant.

It is this truly God-centred person, who himself resisted temptation and therefore empathises fully with what I feel, who has sent his Spirit into me to bring healing. No wonder he said, 'If the Son sets you free, you will be free indeed.' (John 8:36).

Jesus is Lord

Claudius Ptolemy (85–165 AD) was the most influential of Greek astronomers and geographers of his time. He propounded the geocentric theory that taught that the earth was the centre of the universe and all the heavenly bodies, including the sun and moon, revolved around it. Most people throughout Europe accepted this theory unquestioningly for the best part of 1400 years. Then a man named Nicolas Copernicus (1473–1543) eventually came along and claimed that the earth actually went around the sun. All the experts had to do a complete rethink. What a turnaround for everyone!

The same is true with how many people view God. They think that they themselves are the centre of the universe. If there is a God, he somehow revolves around them and is there to call on if the need arises. He's a bit like a spiritual slot-machine when it comes to prayer, and faith doesn't really enter into it very much; if your prayers aren't answered then perhaps there isn't a God after all. I have to say that many Christians aren't a lot better than that. They'll say, 'Jesus is my Lord', but do they really believe it? Is he there to be followed, the Captain who leads the way, who calls us to take up our cross daily in our walk with him? Or are we actually doing things our own way while he rather conveniently fits in, or not as the case may be?

If we really think the world and God revolve around us, then I don't think we can ever expect to find healing and wholeness in our lives. So many self-help therapies begin with the person and end with the person. The kind of healing I'm talking about begins with God and ends with God. My wholeness comes from being within his love and part of what he is doing.

I think it's wonderful whenever anyone becomes a Christian, no matter how old or how young. The angels always rejoice when a sinner repents. However, I'm really glad that I started following Jesus when I was a teenager. You see, they say that teenage years and the early twenties are really the age of adventure. Young people don't really need to be entertained; they need to be given a quest, a mission, an exciting road to travel. Anything else is just trying to fill the hole. No amount of drugs, alcohol, sexual thrills or whatever will really satisfy.

At the time, I don't think I realised what a crucial stage adolescence can be:

> None of us pass through this (adolescent) period totally unscathed. The wounds may have been superficial and easily healed with the passage of time. But some of the traumas of adolescence leave deep wounds from which we may not have fully recovered.
>
> In each stage of development there are several important objectives to be reached. No less important are the developmental tasks of the teenager. As before, if these tasks of not adequately worked through, immature responses and behaviour patterns may result and pose difficulties for the next stage of life.[7]

I was aware of it being a very uncomfortable stage, as I think most adolescents are. Indeed it's a time to grow through as quickly as possible, many would say. It's another of the stages of life where the individual is incredibly self-centred. You only have to consider how long teenagers spend in front of the mirror to realise that!

I wasn't abnormal in that respect, but I'm convinced that the fact I became a Christian during adolescence, the age of adventure, set me up for getting through early adulthood, which proved in my case to be a very difficult stage indeed. I'm convinced it helped that early in my Christian life I adopted a view that God wasn't there to revolve around me, rather the opposite. Jesus was indeed my Captain and my Lord, and I knew my life was not my own. I'm pretty sure that if that had not been the case I would have struggled even to begin to sort out my emotions later on. I was by no means perfect in this, as you've seen throughout this book. At least I had this as a conscious mindset; to a large extent, the subconscious had to do a lot of catching up.

Choice

The whole thing about becoming God-centred is not unlike what we saw much earlier about a therapy like Transactional Analysis. There, once you've been made aware of what's going on in your mind, to adopt a new life position is a matter of the will. It's about deliberately choosing to walk a different path. The same is true about whether you continue being the centre of the universe or revolving around the Lord. The latter is the only sure way of being set free: 'Now that you know these things, you will be blessed if you do them.' (John 13:17). The great difference is that in choosing God's way we open up the possibility of supernatural help, which is something no human therapy can ever hope to offer.

In the end it's all about seeking a balance. On the one hand, we often do need desperately to look within and examine ourselves. Not enough people have self-awareness to the point where they can modify their actions. On the other hand, there comes that point when we have to lift our eyes away from ourselves and find our true worth in the enjoyment of being a child of God: 'I lift up my eyes to the hills – where does my help come from? My help comes from the LORD, the Maker of heaven and earth' (Psalm 121:1–2).

It really does depend on how serious you are about following him and how serious you are therefore of being his child in the full meaning of the word. None of us is perfect, but to fail even to try to move forward both diminishes us and to a degree denies him.

Moving forwards together

Around one in four of the population will suffer from mental health problems at some point in their lives. That statistic involves those who seek medical help; it doesn't include the millions who struggle on while being deeply unhappy because of unresolved emotional situations. Many might not feel things in an intense way; they might even perfect ways of avoiding situations that would create difficulties. Others will just limp on. Some might admit that they've got a bit of an 'inferiority complex', which is how people often describe being 'not OK'. They don't always recognise how much that actually restricts them. It must follow from the statistics that there are many in our churches who could do with some sort of help. The reality is that in any church community where the Holy Spirit is moving and there is growth there will also be a fair smattering of people with mental or emotional needs. As the Spirit opens people up, doing His work of renewing and healing, these needs may become more marked and often be brought out into the open.

My experience is that whenever there are times of intense meeting of the believers with God they are nearly always followed by people needing to talk more about their problems and feelings. Those who avoid an experience of God's power tend to keep their feelings hidden away and protected. However, let's not get hooked on problems. The body of Christ has a job to do. Part of its function is for people to support each other, to listen and to stand alongside each other. But also we are commanded to go into the world and make disciples. The church exists for those who are not yet members of it. We have a message of salvation, healing and wholeness that is to be taken to every human being. We can't do that if we spend all the time dwelling on our own problems.

There will be those reading this book who might not relate to anything I've said. You might even dismiss me as a raving lunatic! Thankfully, there are many people who have had happy upbringings. Their families have not been dysfunctional, and they have been nurtured in a loving environment. Not all parents fight, and thankfully not all parents split up. Those people feel OK in relation to everyone else; they're not driven by competitiveness or feeling they've got something to prove; they're not particularly shy or lacking in confidence; they're reasonably secure in themselves. I'm not suggesting we need to go looking for difficulties where none exists.

Nevertheless, I do believe that true renewal in the Holy Spirit will always involve learning something new about yourself. We've all had to negotiate a real minefield in growing up. If we are to believe the experts, most families are at some stage like boxes with inflated balloons squeezing each other out of existence![8]

Hopefully, a church family can learn not to be like that. We should be able to mature, as long as we can understand our own selves and each other better. If you are experiencing any difficulties with your feelings then I would encourage you to find someone to talk to. They need to be someone who can listen, without judging and without trying to provide quick answers. As Proverbs 20:5 says, 'The purposes of a man's heart are deep waters, but a man of understanding draws them out.' Don't assume that that person needs to be a vicar or minister. At the same time, don't be afraid to seek professional help if necessary. Whatever happens, don't try to 'be strong' and suffer alone.

Finally, let's remember that renewal in the Holy Spirit is a serious business. We often talk about the Spirit being as gentle as a dove, but he is also powerful. He is the force that made us, that breathed life into us in the first place, that raised Jesus from the dead, that can move mountains if he wants to, that stirs the waves and put the stars in space. He is not a safe Spirit! He brings good gifts to God's children, but as I learned all those years ago there is much, much more he wants to do in us.

My journey has not been an easy one, nor is my learning over by a long way. Writing this book has been good in helping me to continue thinking things through. However, my real hope is that my experience might encourage others to face up to themselves a little more. We need reality in our relationships, and usually that can only come when we are honest with ourselves and with each other about the emotions we experience.

Remember, there is always hope. Even if you have sunk to the depths of depression for whatever reason, there is always hope. If you're worried about your children because your own marriage broke up, there is always hope for them, as there was for me. If you feel you're just not moving on in life, there is always hope, as long as you can begin to see things from God's perspective. And what is his perspective? That he loves you more than you can possibly know. There may be times when you feel a stranger to yourself, the 'stranger on the shore' feeling lost. But you're never a stranger to him. When he looks at you he doesn't condemn you, neither for your sin which he is ready to forgive, nor for your sickness which he is longing to heal. Whatever you think about yourself he looks at you as his creation and his child, and he thinks you're great!

Notes

1. John Eldredge, *Wild at Heart*, (Nelson, 2001, p. 126).
2. John Piper, *Brothers, We Are Not Professionals*, (Mentor, 2003, p. 16).
3. Brother Yun, *The Heavenly Man*, (Monarch Books, 2002).
4. John Piper, *Desiring God*, (Inter-Varsity Press, orig. publ. 1986, p. 257).
5. Stuart Lees, *Transforming Life*, (Kingsway Publications, 1997, p. 111).
6. D.M. Lloyd-Jones, *The Christian Warfare*, (Banner of Truth Trust, 1976, p. 90).
7. Mary Pytches, *Yesterday's Child*, (Hodder and Stoughton, 1990, p. 137).
8. See Robin Skynner and John Cleese, *Families and How to Survive Them*, (Methuen, 1983, p. 92).